I LOVE YOU
BUT HOW DO I LIVE WITH YOU?

ALSO BY DES HUNT

What Makes People Tick: Understanding Yourself and Others

How to Sell the Way Your Customer Buys

AWC Solutions Pty Ltd
P.O Box 282, Kensington Park, South Australia 5068
Phone: +61(0)8 8463 1986
Email: info@tick.com.au
Website: www.tick.com.au

I LOVE YOU
BUT HOW DO I LIVE WITH YOU?

How to Understand Yourself and Your Partner

Des Hunt

I Love You – But How Do I Live With You?
How to Understand Yourself and Your Partner

Copyright © 2003 by Des Hunt. All rights reserved.

This 3rd edition published 2014 by
AWC Business Solutions
www.tick.com.au

No part of this publication may be reproduced in any form or by any means, electronic, mechanical, photocopying, recording, or otherwise, without the prior consent and written permission of the author and the publishers.

National Library of Australia
Cataloguing-in-Publication Entry

Hunt, Des J., 1940-.

ISBN: 978-0-9925553-7-5 (sc)
ISBN: 978-0-9925553-6-8 (ebk)

Printed in Australia

Cover design by: Andrew Cole

For my grandchildren

Sam
Ryan
Jane
Morgan
Tim

Who have parents who
understand and love
each other and who
love them

CONTENTS

1   **I LOVE YOU DARLING** 1
Love is Blind / 5
Birds Do It, Bees Do It / 5
If In Doubt, Burn This Book / 6
I Will Love You Forever ... Perhaps / 7
Russian Roulette / 10

2   **WHEN THE HONEYMOON IS OVER** 13
A More Realistic Love Song? / 15
The Relationship Lottery / 17
Shortening the Odds / 18
Men Are From Earth and Women Are From Earth / 21

3   **TOWARDS A BETTER UNDERSTANDING OF HUMAN NATURE** 23
The 5 Basic Principles of Human Nature / 24
What Do People Want? / 24

4   **OUR PERSONALITIES** 29
What Is Personality? / 29
Are People That Predictable? / 29
Do We Change Our Personalities? / 30
How Does Character Differ From Personality? / 30
Can We, Or Do We, Change Our Personalities? / 30
Where Do Our Personalities Come From? / 31

Why Can't You Be More Like Me? / 33
There Ain't No Such Thing As The Perfect Person / 34

5 INTRODUCING THE FOUR BASIC PERSONALITY STYLES 35
The Four Basic Personality Styles / 37
Not Strictly for the Birds / 38
Are There More Than Four Basic Personality Styles? / 39

6 PERSONALITY PORTRAITS 41
Meet The Peacock / 43
Meet The Dove / 51
Meet The Eagle / 58
Meet The Owl / 66
Public Faces / 73
Driving Forces / 74

7 WHAT IS THIS THING CALLED LOVE? 75
Love Is Different Strokes for Different Folks / 77
Going From In-Love to Loving / 78
Real Love Has No Room for Pygmalion Chisels / 78
How We Use Our Pygmalion Chisels / 81
Let the Pygmalion Games Begin! / 83
We All Play Them / 84

8 OUR WINDOWS OF LIFE 87
The View From My Window / 88
Life Views from the Different Windows / 90
You Can Get Almost Anything You Want / 92
Their Reasons / 93
We Are Not Logical Creatures / 95
The Emotional Wants of the Four Styles / 96

9 CONFLICTS AND QUARRELS 99
Self-Defence Mechanisms / 100
Clashing Personalities / 101
Nobody Can Really Upset Us Unless We Let Them / 103
Hates of the Four Styles / 105

10 DO YOU KNOW WHAT REALLY ANNOYS ME? 107
Strengths and Shortcomings / 109
Common Partner Complaints About the Peacock / 111
Common Partner Complaints About the Dove / 112
Common Partner Complaints About the Eagle / 113
Common Partner Complaints About the Owl / 114

11 RELATIONSHIP STRATEGIES 115
Relationship Strategies for Living With the Peacock / 118
Relationship Strategies for Living With the Dove / 1121
Relationship Strategies for Living With the Eagle / 124
Relationship Strategies for Living With the Owl / 127

12 COMMUNICATING 131
Are You Listening To Me? / 132
Why Don't You Talk To Me? / 133
Communication Styles / 135
We Speak a Different Language / 137

13 THE MONEY WARS 141
The Peacock and Money / 143
The Dove and Money / 144
The Eagle and Money / 145
The Owl and Money / 146

14 THE FOUR BASIC STYLES IN A NUTSHELL 149

15 UP CLOSE AND PERSONAL 153
Understanding Your Partner's World / 153
About the Questionnaires That Follow / 154
How To Score the Questionnaire / 154
How I See Myself Questionnaire / 156
How My Partner Sees Me Questionnaire / 157
How I See Myself Questionnaire for Your Partner / 158
How I See My Partner Questionnaire / 159
How My Friends See Me Questionnaire / 160
How My Friends See Me Questionnaire for Your Partner / 161
About the Profile Descriptions / 162
A Guide to the Galaxy / 162
Eight Out of Ten Ain't Bad / 162

16 THE 16 PARTNER STYLES 163
Quick Index to the 16 Partner Styles / 164
The Extreme Peacock Partner / 166
The Peacock-Dove Partner / 175
The Peacock-Eagle Partner / 183
The Peacock-Owl Partner / 190
The Extreme Dove Partner / 195
The Dove-Peacock Partner / 202
The Dove-Eagle Partner / 209
The Dove-Owl Partner / 214
The Extreme Eagle Partner / 220
The Eagle-Peacock Partner / 227
The Eagle-Dove Partner / 235
The Eagle-Owl Partner / 240
The Extreme Owl Partner / 247
The Owl-Peacock Partner / 253
The Owl-Dove Partner / 258
The Owl-Eagle Partner / 264

17 VIVA LA DIFFERENCE! 271
Let's Applaud the Peacock / 271
Let's Care for the Dove / 272
Let's Admire the Eagle / 272
Let's Respect the Owl / 272

18 LIVING AND LOVING FOR LIFE 273
The BDBADA Road / 273
Where Are the Goalposts? / 275
A Compass for the Journey / 276
A Relationship Can Be Hard Work / 278
The Is No Such Thing as a Little Thing / 279
You Have to Accentuate the Positive / 279
I Cannot Live Without You / 280
To Be Happily Married / 282
Choices Are Our Chisels / 282
Love Is a Choice / 284

19 THE RULES OF THE GAME OF LIFE 285

Acknowledgements / 287

1

I LOVE YOU DARLING

"I think about you all the time. I think about you day and night. Darling, I just can't live without you."

"Me too."

"I do"

Jason, do you take Belinda to be your wife, and do you solemnly promise to love, honour and cherish her, and that forsaking all others for her alone, you will perform unto her all the duties that a husband owes to his wife until God by death shall separate you?

I, Belinda, take you, Jason, to be my husband. And I promise and covenant before God and these witnesses to be your loving and faithful wife – in plenty and in want, in joy and in sorrow, in sickness and in health – as long as we both shall live.

"I Can't"

For God's sake woman, do you have to fill up all the bathroom cabinet with your crap?"

"You can talk! What about you? You leave your bristles in the basin after you shave — you never clean it up! And while we're on the subject of the bathroom, when will you ever learn to put the toilet lid down?"

The honeymoon is over.

How does "I do" become "I can't"?

How did "Darling, I just can't live without you," become "How the hell am I going to live with you"?

Most marriages are happy.

***It's trying to live together
after that can cause
all the problems!***

LOVE IS BLIND

"How the hell am I going to live with you?"

It sounds like an echo of what my dear old dad once said to me after having an interchange with my mother as he retreated to the quiet solitude of his beloved back shed. (I was a war baby. As soon as I was born, my parents started fighting!)

He said: "Son, don't marry somebody you can't live without, marry somebody you can bloody well live with!"

As was usual for dad, it was good advice. But like most things in life, it's easier said than done.

When the heart is pounding, when you are in the grip of mad passionate love, with stars in your eyes and your head in the clouds, plus all the other well-worn clichés used to describe romantic love, how can you keep your feet on the ground? How do you know whether or not you can live with your lover?

As they say in the classics 'Love is blind'.

Romantic love is not only blind; it's also deaf and dumb! That's why romantic love has been described as, "The triumph of imagination over intelligence"!

Don't get me wrong, I'm all for romantic love.

But you have to admit that when the hormones are in a state of chaos, it's not the greatest time to be thinking about making life-long decisions.

BIRDS DO IT, BEES DO IT

Birds do it, bees do it, we all do it — it's called the Mating Game.

When boy meets girl and they fall in love, it's a sexual attraction thing. It's about the dance of the hormones. When testosterone meets oestrogen anything can happen. That's why a man gives his penis a name — He doesn't want a stranger making 99 per cent of his decisions!

Falling in love is about the hormones doing a really good job of exactly what they were invented for — the survival of the species. It's what keeps us populating the planet. It's a good set up and I have no problems with it what so ever. In fact I think it's a rather good idea all round.

Romantic Love is nature's way of making sure we get our things together, so to speak. And for the dance of the hormones to really work properly it has to give the illusion that it is going to last forever. It has to give the impression that we will be 'in love forever', that we will 'live happily ever after', just like in the fairy tales and the old movies, and in just about any love song you like to name, except for country and western songs — they're more about what happens after the Romantic period has come to an end.

For those who like to get technical, according to Professor Cindy Hazen of Cornell University, who conducted five thousand interviews and medical tests across thirty-seven different cultures, romantic love lasts around two years and is induced by a conditioned release of dopamine phenyl ethylamine and oxytocin. It almost sounds toxic, doesn't it!

In other words, romantic Love is about sex. And sex is good. A little coitus never hoitus as they say. In fact, we Aussies are rather fond of it. According to an international survey conducted by condom-maker Durex, we are the world's most frequent lovers after the French. We have sex on average 116 times a year compared with the international average of 109. I can't help but think that somebody out there is helping my average a bit!

It's OK to be good in bed because that's where we are going to spend about a third of our lives, but irrespective of how much we like sex, no matter how you cut it, most of that time is going to be spent sleeping.

We are also going to have thousands of breakfasts together. There is nothing like how we look at breakfast to bring us back to reality, not to mention all those lazy Sunday mornings letting it all hang out in trackkies and shorts.

As the new wife said to her husband as she looked at him one Sunday morning two months after they were married, "I know I married you for better or for worse — but this is bloody ridiculous!"

IF IN DOUBT, BURN THIS BOOK

I just had a sudden thought that you might think, that I think, that I know all the answers.

Let me quickly assure you that I don't — far from it.

As I've gotten older, I've discovered that just when I think I've got all the answers they change the questions on me. I have also discovered that only fools can be certain. It takes wisdom to be confused.

It is not my intention to try and tell you how to live your life. I have enough trouble trying to live my own. What I will try and do is share some thoughts and experiences with you. As Oscar Wilde once said, "Experience is the name everyone gives their mistakes." And I've made plenty of them!

In fact, my original intention for writing this book was to put my thoughts down as a guide for my grandchildren — a readership of five people.

The bottom line is this; if at any time I sound as if I'm preaching, or telling you how to live your life, shut the book and burn it. There are too many people out there already trying to do that without me getting in on the act.

I WILL LOVE YOU FOREVER ..PERHAPS

There is an old song that has the line, "What is this thing called love"?

It's not a bad question really — although the song never answered the question. But there is one thing for sure — we certainly use the word 'love' loosely.

"Don't you just love it."

"I love your shoes."

"I love it when you do that."

We 'fall in love' daily. We fall in love with people; we fall in love with clothes; we fall in love with cars; we fall in love with all sorts of things. Some of us even fall in love with love itself.

And we can 'fall out of love' just as quickly. Why? Because 'being in love', romantic love, is always a temporary thing. Come on, let's be honest, sooner or later the heat and passion of the romance starts to fade. There is nothing more certain in life (except maybe death and taxes), than the heat and passion eventually cooling.

As I said earlier, research shows that Romantic Love lasts around two years before the flame starts to die.

Although if you look at the divorce rate in Hollywood, it would seem that theirs may be a little shorter!

After the groggy influence of hormone-driven romantic love has cooled: When that funny little mannerism your lover has, that you saw through romantic eyes, and thought so cute, suddenly starts to drive you nuts; after the wedding album has been seen by just about everybody you can possibly show and is finally put away; when the bills start coming in; when he starts leaving his socks all over the place, and when she takes over the bathroom. "It's that time", as my dear old dad used to say (he had a saying for almost any occasion), "When the flowers stop and the farting starts."

It's that time when the honeymoon is over and reality sets in. And for many couples it can be that time when they look at each other and wonder how the hell they got there in the first place — leave alone how they are going to live together!

It can be like the old joke that goes, "After we got married, we found that the only thing we had in common with each other was that we were both married on the same day!"

The current trend is towards shorter honeymoons, but more of them!

RUSSIAN ROULETTE

I was going to say that finding a partner we can live with for life is like playing Russian Roulette.

But on second thoughts, playing Russian Roulette offers better odds than marriage. The statistics show that around one in two marriages end in divorce. That's half. That's odds of one in two. That's lousy odds. Russian Roulette has odds of one in six!

And the incredible thing is that the statistics also show that the odds of a second marriage being any more successful than the first are not much better.

Of course the figures don't take into account all those unhappy marriages that are 'staying together for the sake of the kids'. (While on this subject; years of surveys show that while divorce is bad for children, they also show that children who grow up within a loveless marriage — with emotional static and conflict the order of the day — can be just as painfully affected in later life as those who experienced a painful divorce of their parents).

The figures also do not take into account all those couples who try living together and eventually break up. Interestingly enough the latest research also shows that people who live together before they get married have a higher divorce rate than the couples who don't. So we can't say the principle of 'try before you buy' works all that well as a guide to whether or not a relationship will last the distance either.

These statistics show us that the two major causes of marriage break-up are men and women!

As an optimist, (I generally see the glass as half full. But then again, it depends on whether I'm drinking or pouring!), so looking at the other side of the coin, we also have to keep in mind that half of all Australian marriages last a lifetime. Therefore, it would seem that half of us are either lucky, or have worked out (and it ain't easy) how to make a relationship work.

Or then again, perhaps half the couples who are married would like to sit down and play their wedding video backwards so that they can see themselves single again!

The bottom line is that at least half of us are either lousy at picking a partner we can love for life, or we haven't worked out not only how to love, but more importantly, how to *live with* a partner for life. Which, I suppose, is what my dear old dad was on about.

Romantic Love is often responsible for many of us marrying the wrong person.

2

WHEN THE HONEYMOON IS OVER

According to the figures then, there is around a 50/50 chance that after the honeymoon is over, when the libido returns to room temperature and the hormones have gone from dancing to walking, we may wake up one morning to find that we have married the wrong person!

And why shouldn't we? Let's face it, the odds are better than even that we are just as likely to fall in love with somebody we are hopelessly ill-matched with, as we are with somebody we are compatible with.

The reason they say that 'love is blind', is because romantic love blinds us to what makes us different, or it certainly hides the differences, and if we're not careful, it can mask and hide the very differences that could kill a long-term relationship.

In a way, love really is blind. Without wanting to get into too much psycho-talk, the problem we can have (especially when we are in love) is what the psychologists call 'Projection'. It's a natural thing — we all do it — no one can escape it.

Projection happens because we are naturally inclined to believe that the world is as we see it. We believe that people are who we imagine them to be. When we are in love, we project (and see) all the things we imagine (and want) someone to be — we project and see an ideal (but not realistic) picture.

Later, when we get to know them better, we generally discover that they are quite different from the way we thought. If the person is not particularly close, it doesn't worry us too much. But if it happens to be our lover, we are devastated. We suddenly find we are in a relationship with a person who no longer fits the picture we fell in love with.

The thing is, before we're married, when we're in love, we feel as one. We do everything as one. We think as one. We are one. 'Nothing can tear us apart', as the song goes. But after the passion of the romantic period is over, and reality inevitably settles in, we find that we have become two separate individuals again, with entirely different personalities.

As they say: "Love is the delusion that one person is better than another."

When we feel as one, it's what psychology calls 'Identification'. In a way it's a lot like 'empathy', but 'Identification' means that we literally and totally identify with somebody else. "They're exactly like me." "I can relate exactly with what you're feeling." With Identification there is no separation between me and the other person. We are two peas in a pod. You are me — I am you. What's good for me must be good for you. Many relationships have run aground on this mistaken notion of 'oneness'.

As time goes by, we notice that our loved one isn't quite as perfect as we thought. We start to notice all those irritatingly bad habits we hadn't noticed before. With a thud we discover that our soul mate, our lover, the person we thought was so perfect, the person we thought was so compatible with us, all of a sudden has a whole different set of habits, ideas, opinions and aims from our own.

Perhaps we need to rewrite some of those love songs to make them more realistic.

A MORE REALISTIC LOVE SONG?

Perhaps a more realistic love song would go something like this:

The sun is shining and the birds are singing,
   I'm dressed in white; the church bells are ringing;
For today my love we become husband and wife,
   And we'll pledge our vows that will last for life.

Today's the day that I become your bride,
   And our love will go on like the raging tide.
We'll build a lovely house just near the hills;
   Then we'll scrimp and save to pay the bills.

The mortgage will kill us and cause us tears,
   We'll both have to work for years and years,
And if we want to live in a certain style;
   We can forget having kids for quite a while.

When we do have kids, there's one thing for sure,
   Until they're twenty they'll keep us poor.
We'll need clothes and shoes to put on their feet;
   I'll get a part time job to make ends meet.

We'll work our bums off, and after several years,
   Wonder if it was worth all the blood, sweat and tears.
We'll watch TV; perhaps we won't talk like we did,
   Because we'll both be too tired just making a quid.

Life will push us and shove us, try to tear us apart,
   Our friendship will be nothing like it was at the start,
But the battles of life won't be our biggest dangers,
   Our real battle will be not to become total strangers.

If we can weather the storms that life has to give,
   We can stay true lovers for as long as we live.
It's important as we travel life's twists and bends,
   To be not only lovers — but life-long friends.

Picking the right partner works out at 2 to 1 odds.

But if you're lucky you can pick a favourite.

THE RELATIONSHIP LOTTERY

Before we go on, now might be a good time to give you some background on myself. After all, up until now we hardly know each other, but then again, that has never stopped me from talking to strangers before! By the time you have finished reading this book I hope that we will be far from being strangers.

My wife Val was seventeen and I was eighteen when we married. We were both still kids, really. I remember there was a song in the 'Top 40 Hits' at the time that went along the lines of, "She was only seventeen and he was one year more. She loved him with all her heart and he the girl adored..." How romantic it was. It was 'our song'. It fitted us perfectly — ain't love grand!

The actual reality though wasn't quite so perfect or grand. When we were married I was a third year apprentice carpenter being paid around a third of the then average weekly wage. Steak was rare, and I don't mean the way we ate it, I mean it was a rarity to have. We quickly learnt (or tried) to live on apprenticeship wages and had to for the next three years. You learn to love Vegemite sandwiches — often. We had our two daughters by the time we were both twenty. Boy, did that add a whole new perspective to our lives and to our relationship.

A lot of water has flowed under the proverbial bridge since then — oceans of it. We have now been married for over forty years and are the proud grandparents of five grandchildren. Our eldest daughter, Tracy has two, and my youngest daughter, Julie has three. We have two great sons-in-law, Glen and Mark, and as I write this, life is being good to us.

To return to the relationship between Val and me; our life together has been one of blissful love and affection. Our romance has just got stronger and stronger as the years have gone by. We have never had a disagreement or an argument. We have never wanted to ever be apart. It has been a marriage made in Heaven.

Now, if you really believe all that rubbish, I know a bloke who can help you invest in some nice cheap building blocks in far North Queensland. He likes you to go up and have a look at them during the dry season — and to bring your money with you when you come. Or you may be interested in a letter I got out of the blue about an investment opportunity in Nigeria...

The truth is that we quickly discovered that real life was a far cry from what they sang about in the love songs.

It would be great to say that our marriage really was made in Heaven, that as young as we were, we chose each other for the qualities we admired in each other. It would be great to say that, but the facts of the matter are quite different. The truth is that when my wife met me she couldn't stand me. (I have never understood this considering how intelligent, handsome and charming I was). And I was attracted to Val because she had great legs, great boobs, and big brown eyes, all of which are terribly important qualities on which to base a life-long relationship!

Let me assure you that very early in the piece there were times when we both secretly had a look at our marriage certificate to see if there was an escape clause!

But as it turned out, luck played a hand. I believe that fate stepped in to our lives and played a big part. Not the fate of romance novels, nor the fate of some divine intervention, but fate like in a lottery; the fate of two quite different personalities meeting, loving, marrying and eventually — eventually that is — learning to live together.

Whatever this fate may be called, I bless it for leading me, (an Eagle/Peacock personality; confident, assertive, independent: a doer) to meet and marry my wife Val, (a Dove/Owl personality; calm, even-tempered, practical: a supporter).

It was pure 'lottery luck' and it happened twenty years before I even thought about personality styles, leave alone start to study and write about them.

SHORTENING THE ODDS

One of the main reasons for writing this book is that I believe we can greatly increase the odds in the 'Relationship Lottery' in our favour.

Firstly, I believe that understanding one's self is imperative to having a happy and lasting relationship.

Secondly, I believe that we can reduce many of the heartaches and tensions that a seeming 'mismatch' (or even a 'good match') can cause, through having a better understanding of our partner's (or potential partner's) inner world — their personality style. And through this understanding, rather than getting frustrated by the tensions that the differences can cause, we can instead respect, appreciate and simply enjoy the differences and get on with loving and living with each other.

Thirdly, I believe that we waste so much time and effort in our relationships struggling to make our partners agree with us when agreement is nowhere near as important as understanding. Because, when we understand each other, there is no need to agree. When we understand each other, we can agree to disagree without becoming disagreeable. And the more we know about our partner's inner world and life-view, the better our chances will be of avoiding the need to have to agree.

Fourthly, I believe that 'loving' is unconditional. As soon as we put conditions on our love, as soon as we start to play the 'Pygmalion Game,' that is, attempt to make our partners conform to how we think they should think and act, then our love is lessened by those conditions. Real love is about letting our partners be just who they are without any 'help' from us.

Finally, I believe that 'real love' is a matter of choice, not luck, nor a feeling that 'just happens'. Real love is as much an act of the brain as it is a feeling of the heart. We can choose to love, or we can choose not to love. The choice is always ours to make. And the choice we make, one way or the other, will dictate just how happy, or unhappy, we are going to be.

Men and women are not from different planets.

MEN ARE FROM EARTH AND WOMEN ARE FROM EARTH

Before we go any further, let's clear up this business of men and women being from different planets.

Irrespective of what some of the American best selling pop psychologists would have us believe, it has nothing to do with coming from different parts of the solar system. Except perhaps for the difference in our hormonal brain wiring, we are strikingly similar in personality traits. There are just as many women Eagles out there, as there are men Doves and vice versa.

This is one of the reasons why many couples had problems with the book, *Men Are From Mars And Women Are From Venus*. When they read the book they found that the man in the relationship better fitted the so-called 'feminine traits' and the woman the 'masculine traits'. The reason for their confusion was that it has nothing to do with gender and everything to do with personality.

While on the same subject, the book, *Why Men Don't Listen and Women Can't Read Maps* is just as misleading. Men Doves are excellent listeners, and women Owls are great map-readers. Again, it's not a gender issue — it's a personality thing.

Continuing on the same subject, I have just finished reading an article titled, *What Sex Is Your Brain?* The article contains a questionnaire to fill in along with a diagram which, when plotted based on the answers to the questionnaire, reveals what type of brain you have. It shows diagrams of a 'Typically Female Brain' and a 'Typically Male Brain'.

On answering the questions and then plotting my score I've just discovered that I'm a female.

And considering the way I'm built, that's a bit of a worry!

One more time with feeling:

It's not a gender thing — it's a personality thing.

But before we get into the personality thing, let's get to know our fellow human beings a bit better. Let's have a look at some basic principles of human nature.

People do things for their reasons, not yours, and they always will.

3

TOWARDS A BETTER UNDERSTANDING OF HUMAN NATURE

We could spend quite a bit of time here talking about some in-depth psychology, and I could show off with some pretty fancy psycho-babble words.
That is the last thing I intend to do.
Rather, what I will do is share with you the 5 basic principles of human nature, and what drives it that I have found to be an invaluable guide when it comes to dealing with people.

Here they are.

THE 5 BASIC PRINCIPLES OF HUMAN NATURE

1. Human beings are self-centred creatures — we think about ourselves 98% of the time.

2. We are not logical. Nobody has ever made a truly logical decision to do anything.

3. People do things for emotional reasons then justify it with logic. We make the facts fit our fictions.

4. People do things for their reasons, not yours, and they always will. Therefore, If you are going to bet on the human race, always back self-interest to win.

5. You can get almost anything you want by giving people what they want.

WHAT DO PEOPLE WANT?

(a) To live and survive.

(b) Food, shelter, safety and sex.

(c) Certainty and predictability.

(d) Love, friendship and belonging.

(e) Recognition, praise and applause.

(f) Control, authority and power.

And for some:

(g) To be all we are capable of being.

Marketers appeal to these wants and businesses make billions of dollars satisfying them.

Let's take a closer look at them:

(a) To live and survive.

(b) Food, shelter, safety and sex.

These are the basic 'animal' wants that both humans and animals share. Once these wants are satisfied, they do not motivate us until the need for them again arises.

Then we have our human psychological wants:

(c) Certainty and predictability.

(d) Love, friendship and belonging.

(e) Recognition, praise and applause.

(f) Control, authority and power.

These psychological wants are rarely, if ever, satisfied. We just can't seem to get enough of whichever one spins our wheels. For example:

(c) Certainty and predictability.

This want ranges from knowing our jobs are secure to never wanting the world to change. We all like a bit of certainty and predictability in our lives, but for the Owl-type personality, who we will meet in the next chapter, they are 'addicted' to it. They just can't get enough of it.

(d) Love, friendship and belonging.

This want ranges from wanting our partner and children to love us, to wanting the whole world to love us. We all like to be liked and have a bit of loving, but for the Dove-type personality, who we will also meet in the next chapter, it is a driving obsession. They cannot live without it.

(e) Recognition, praise and applause.

This want ranges from being told how much we are appreciated to winning an Academy Award. We all like a bit of recognition now and again, but the Peacock-personality, who we will also meet in the next chapter, is totally hooked on it. It dictates almost everything they do.

(f) Control, authority and power.

This want ranges from telling people what to do to wanting to rule the world. We all like a bit of control in our lives, but to the Eagle personality, who we will also meet in the next chapter, they are possessed by it. It rules their lives.

(g) To be all we can be.

This is the getting of wisdom. It is the pursuit of rising above the basic psychological needs. It is striving to be all we can be. Some make it. Some never start the journey.

We will revisit these principles and needs in later chapters, but for now, let's have a look at understanding the four basic personalities styles.

Our personalities are simply in-built habits of thinking, feeling and acting.

*I will always return to
where I can be me.*

4

OUR PERSONALITIES

The following are some of the questions, along with my answers, that people who attend my 'What Makes People Tick' seminars and workshops invariably ask me about personality.

Please keep in mind that here, and at all times throughout this book, I am talking about *normal* people (if there is any such thing). In other words, people who have no obvious psychological problems.

WHAT IS PERSONALITY?

Our personalities are simply in-built habits of the way we think, feel and act.

ARE PEOPLE THAT PREDICTABLE?

Yes. Depending on our personality style, the way we think, feel and act in a given situation is highly predictable.

DO WE CHANGE OUR PERSONALITIES?

In our day-to-day lives the world forces us to be different people at different times; we are forced to 'play the part'. That's life. But it is always uncomfortable playing a part for too long. Sooner or later, (and it's normally sooner than later), we have to return to our comfort zone — to our personality style — where 'I can just be me'. Much of our stress (both at home and at work) is caused through being out of our comfort zones for too long and too often. That is when you get ulcers. Ulcers don't come from what you eat — they come from what's eating you.

HOW DOES 'CHARACTER' DIFFER FROM 'PERSONALITY'?

Character is conditioning. Our character is shaped (conditioned) in our early years. It is influenced by our parents, our siblings, our relatives, our friends, our religion, our surroundings and the like. It is especially and strongly influenced from the age of nought to seven. Our conditioning helps form our beliefs and value system. (As an example, research shows that most of us vote for the same political party as our parents). Character and personality both influence the decisions we make. But having said that, when it comes to a struggle between our character and our personality, our personality will win — every time.

CAN WE, OR DO WE, CHANGE OUR PERSONALITIES?

The first short answer is no. The next short answer is; why would you want to? The long answer is that when we suffer a significant emotional event, like the death of a loved one for instance, or even the loss of a job, or a divorce, we can go through a grieving period and become 'a different person'.

But after a period of time, (and perhaps a little more mature and wiser) we return to being 'the same old person we were'.

I find this question normally contains the seed of another question, which is, "How can I become more assertive, or sensitive, or impulsive, or whatever; how can I strengthen what I perceive as a weakness in myself?" The short answer to this one is; be aware of it first. Know thyself. We are unlikely to change until we see ourselves as we truly are. Self-knowledge is the first step to personal development. Knowing your personality style and recognising your in-built habits is a giant leap in that direction. Also, any relationship you have is going to be that much harder if you don't know yourself well. And until you understand yourself, it is impossible to understand somebody else.

WHERE DO OUR PERSONALITIES COME FROM?

The academics are going to hate this answer, but after 30 years of studying and observing personality styles, I now believe that our personalities are genetic, that they are part of our DNA. I am convinced that our personalities are as genetically inherited from our parents, as are the features of our face. In other words, we have as much choice about our personality as we do about the shape of our body, or the sound of our voice.

How often have you heard the comments: "He's a chip off the old block, even his mannerisms are the same." "She even walks and talks like..."

So, like inheriting a mixture of our mother and father's features, I also believe that we inherit a mixture of our mother and father's personality styles as well. And like similar physical features, one or the other of our mother's, or father's, personality style may dominate.

The bottom line is that our personality is not something we choose, nor is it changeable. So, in any relationship we have a simple (but not so easy) choice. We can either accept our partner's personality or not. And if we choose not to, then we are in for a hard ride.

We cannot change our partner's personality, no matter what we do. All the coaxing, all the coercion, all the criticism, all the nagging, all the gentle encouragement to change him or her will be a fruitless no-win game. Yet many of us attempt to do just that. And when we do, we lose.

Playing the game of "Why Can't You Be More Like Me?" is a no-win game.

There are no exceptions to this rule.

It has been said that a single person is somebody who never finds out how many faults they have.

WHY CAN'T YOU BE MORE LIKE ME?

There is an old (and rather sexist) joke that says a woman thinks about three things in the church as she walks down the aisle during her wedding: 'Aisle, altar, hymn.' (I'll alter him).

It is sexist because research shows that most of us, both men and women, attempt to mould our partners into our way of thinking. We try to create a mirror image of ourselves in our partner. In other words, we play the 'Pygmalion Game'.

Let me explain what I mean.

The play, and later the movie *My Fair Lady* ("Why can't a woman be more like a man?") was based on the book *Pygmalion* written by George Bernard Shaw in 1913.

Shaw based his story on the Greek myth of Pygmalion. Pygmalion, so the myth goes, was the King of Cyprus who searched for the perfect woman but couldn't find one. He then set out to lovingly carve out of a block of ivory his image of the perfect woman. When he had finished his creation he fell in love with it, caressing and kissing the statue.

His adoration soon turned to tears and frustration when the cold ivory statue gave no response. But, like all good stories, it has a happy ending with the god of love, Aphrodite, breathing life into the statue and bringing her to life. The story ends with Pygmalion marrying his perfect woman.

It's a great myth, and that is all it is — a myth. In the world of reality there is no Aphrodite.

But there are plenty of Pygmalions.

All of us in some way are Pygmalions. Rather than accepting our loved ones' perfectly human differences and seeing them as normal for their personality style, we see them as faults and imperfections. We then take up our Pygmalion chisels of all shapes and sizes and start to sculpt — criticising, brow-beating, bullying, whining, giving the silent treatment, and using guilt and flattery.

But the Pygmalion Game is always a no-win project because even if we 'succeed' we fail. When we try to sculpt, mould and change our partner into our way of thinking, when we try to make them who they are not, we lose some of the very qualities that attracted us to them in the first place — or we lose them completely.

As a friend of mine once said:

"The way my husband finds fault with me you'd think there was a reward!"

It's only natural (actually, it's unnatural) that we would like our loved ones to be perfect, but there are no perfect people. Just people.

THERE AIN'T NO SUCH THING AS THE PERFECT PERSON

The most perfect wife in the world belongs to the man next door!

All jokes aside, we spend a hell of a lot of our lives trying to please other people.

> We try to be the perfect wife, but there are no perfect husbands.
> We try to be the perfect husband, but there are no perfect wives.
> We try to be the perfect parent, but there are no perfect kids.
> We try to be the perfect child, but there are no perfect parents.
> We try to be the perfect employee, but there are no perfect bosses.
> We try to be the perfect mate, but there are no perfect mates.
> We try to be the perfect person, but there are no perfect people.

We are only human. And our personalities are a big part of what makes us human and far from being perfect.

To prove the point, let's meet the four basic personality styles: The Peacock, The Dove, The Eagle, and The Owl.

5

INTRODUCING THE FOUR BASIC PERSONALITY STYLES

*The difference between
love and hate is
understanding.*

It takes all kinds to make a world.

THE FOUR BASIC PERSONALITY STYLES

The Peacock

G'Day, I'm a Peacock. I reckon life is about living and having fun. I can talk the leg off a chair, but I hate listening. I'm the life of the party when I'm up, or bloody awful to live with when I'm down. I'm the original dummy-spitter when I'm angry. Lucky I'm so popular. I can drive you nuts wanting to be the centre of attention all the time.

The Dove

Hello, I'm a Dove and I feel that life is about caring for others. People are important and we all need to help each other. If we did, what a beautiful world it would be. I'm quiet and quite bashful and modest. The last thing I want to do is to offend anyone or hurt anyone's feelings. And I can drive you nuts with my niceness.

The Eagle

I don't have time for this stuff. I have things to do. Who cares what makes people tick. If everybody just got on with what they should be doing instead of navel gazing we might get something done around here. You might have gathered by now that I like to be the boss. I can drive you batty wanting to be in charge of things all the time. But that's your problem, not mine.

The Owl

Hello. I'm an Owl and I take life very seriously. You have to be cautious and on your guard. There must be law and order, otherwise who knows what would happen. Decisions must be thought through carefully. One must use knowledge and logic, not emotions when making decisions. I can drive you crazy with my conservative and cautious approach.

NOT STRICTLY FOR THE BIRDS

In my seminars I have found that most people relate instantly with what the birds symbolise, and have fun doing it. It also helps to keep gender out of the way. Also a picture, as they say, is worth a thousand words. Words are those things we use to confuse each other, so the less used, the better. And since writing the book *What Makes People Tick — How to Understand Yourself and Others*, where I used the bird symbols, the feedback has been very positive. So, when you're on a good thing — stick to it!

When I first came up with the idea of using birds to depict the four basic personality styles, I imagined the following:

The Peacock is a colourful and showy bird, it likes to strut its stuff and be admired and if you don't notice it, will spread its beautiful tail feathers so that you do. The 'human Peacock' personality fits this description to a tee.

The Dove is a gentle bird. It is symbolised as the bird of peace. It is quiet, unobtrusive, and most Doves mate for life. The 'human Dove' personality fits this description well.

The Eagle is a no-nonsense bird. Its vision is acute. It sees what it wants from kilometres away, and then goes toward its target with unwavering energy and accuracy. The 'human Eagle' personality fits this description perfectly.

The Owl is a wise bird. It has large eyes, which sees every detail. It likes to see, but not be seen. It never flies too far away from its habitat. It is a creature of habit. The 'human Owl' personality fits this description more than well.

So, you can see that the birds are not strictly for the birds.

ARE THERE MORE THAN FOUR BASIC PERSONALITIES?

The brief answer is yes — and no.

The long answer is that ever since people started to study human nature, and the writings go back to the ancient Greeks with Plato, Aristotle, Galen and Hippocrates through to Carl Jung 1700 years later, right through to the present time, four quite distinct patterns of human behaviour have been consistently recognised.

Simply put, many hundreds of years of studying human nature tell us that there are four distinct and preferred ways of operating with the world which different people find comfortable to use — hence the four basic comfort zones, or personality styles, or temperaments.

Each of these four basic personality styles has in-built habits of thinking and acting which people use in order to make sense out of the world they live in.

Most of us have a bit of each personality style in us. We are a combination of the four styles. But we generally dominate in only two. In fact some of us dominate in only one. I refer to these later as the 'Extreme' styles.

As I have said before, the world forces us to be different people at different times. We are forced to 'play a role'. But it is always uncomfortable being out of our comfort zone (our natural personality style) for too long. Sooner or later, and it's normally sooner, we return to where we feel comfortable — to our comfort zone — to our natural personality style in order to 'just be ourselves'.

Later in the book there are some questionnaires to help you identify your personality style and that of your partner. These are then followed by a full description of the sixteen combinations of the four basic personality styles.

But we'll look at that later.

For now, let's first get to know the four basic personality styles.

*Somewhere or other,
you have met them
all before.*

6

PERSONALITY PORTRAITS

The Peacock

The Dove

The Eagle

The Owl

"What's the point of doing anything worthwhile if there's nobody watching?"

The Anthem of the Peacock

The Peacock

MEET THE PEACOCK

Described by some as outgoing, talkative, energetic and flamboyant, and by others as superficial and self-indulgent, loud and a show-off, the Peacock is driven by the need for recognition, praise and applause. They love it. They just can't get enough of it.

They are socially outgoing, confident, friendly and talkative. They are high-energy people — the way they talk, the way they walk, the way they move — everything is done with energy and exuberance. They like being excited and exciting others. They are the ultimate extroverts.

When they talk, it's fast. They use lots of facial expression, gesture with theatrical flair and use dramatic body language. They are always up with, and use, the latest jargon and in-words. When explaining or describing something they tend to use word pictures and colourful phrases. When they are talking to you, they will use your name more than they need to. Their conversations quickly skip from one topic to another often leaving you wondering what the Hell they are talking about!

They normally dress to impress. Their clothes can be quite colourful (they love red) and quite flamboyant, and always fashionable — they wouldn't be caught dead wearing anything that may be out of fashion. They also tend to wear 'impressive' jewellery (usually lots of it) and other 'impressive' fashion accessories. To the Peacock, 'Nothing Succeeds Like Excess!'

Their cars, (which they drive too fast), are usually 'look-at-me-cars' and invariably red. Or certainly a colour that stands out from the crowd, and they normally have personalised number plates. A secret dream of the Peacock (perhaps not a secret, because they can't keep one!) is to own the latest Porsche — soft-top — red with mag wheels, and with personalised number plates, of course.

They are part of the in-crowd — or would like to be. They are super-cool — or would like to be. They are up with the latest in-places — or would like to be. They are the trendsetters — or would like to be. And they live life in the fast lane — or would like to.

Peacocks are invariably exuberant, vivacious and glamorous. And it's amazing how many of them are physically attractive. And many of them keep themselves attractive and in trim (and looking good) by exercising, jogging and the like. At the gym, they'll be the ones checking themselves out in the mirror as they do their workouts. As they get older, plastic surgery is quite often on the agenda.

They have an amazing ability to instinctively adapt to changing situations and to the company they are with at the time. They are social chameleons. Risk takers one and all, they live by their wits. Like the proverbial cat, no matter what happens to them they tend to land on their feet.

Impetuous, easygoing and playful, as well as confident, cocky, and charming, they are the entertainers, the rascals, the actors and the con artists, or almost anything else they like to apply their talents to.

The Peacock is bright, optimistic and cheerful with a joy for living. They want life to be fun; they want to have a good time. They approach life as a game that shouldn't be taken too seriously. To the Peacock life is an adventure — a smorgasbord filled with variety. They live for the now moment and let tomorrow take care of itself. They are not preoccupied with what happened yesterday. What is done is done. Tomorrow is another day.

Their life is a constant search for excitement, adventure, change, novelty and variety. They hate being bored. And boredom to the Peacock is anything that has a regimented and constant routine to it — a boring sameness. If they are forced to do a job that is regimented and boring, they will try to turn it into a form of play if they can.

To the Peacocks, all the world is a stage. They are the natural entertainers, actors and talkers of the world. As mentioned before, their biggest dream, and the one that drives almost everything they do, is to have *recognition, praise, applause and popularity* — they want to be famous. Or at least they want you to notice them.

In the movie *To Die For*, Nicole Kidman playing the part of a Peacock in full flight, says a classic line which is the anthem of all Peacocks; "What's the point of doing anything worthwhile if there's nobody watching?"

Because of their constant need for recognition, popularity and fame (which is more like a burning desire), they will strive for high achievement in a given field, which in turn will give them the recognition they so desperately seek. And because Peacocks are also natural risk-takers and love to take chances and push their luck, many of them do achieve their dream of fame. The world of acting and modelling is full of Peacocks who have made it and are now strutting their stuff for all the world to see. Peacock heaven!

They often find careers as actors, models, artists, comedians, musicians, writers, cartoonists, designers, architects, salespeople, advertising copywriters, explorers and adventurers; that is, anything that offers them a chance to use their vivid imagination, helps them avoid the boredom of sameness, and gains them recognition, fame and popularity. You'll also see many of them on the professional tennis circuit and sport in general. They have superb eye-to-ball coordination, as they do the natural artistic talent to harmoniously blend sights, sounds and colours.

Good humoured, talkative and entertaining, they can be the life of the party. When they laugh it's hearty and loud — everyone hears them. They have an almost child-like sense of fun — they are the party animals. Impulsive, energetic and impetuous, they enjoy life to the hilt. They can turn any event into a party. And they are certainly not interested in what the neighbours think!

Impatient as well as impulsive (they are the ultimate impulse buyers), they hate waiting for anything. To the Peacock, waiting is mental torture. They want it — and they want it now!

A big dislike is being lonely. They need people around them, someone to talk to. Talking is like oxygen to the Peacock. That is why it can be excruciatingly painful for a Peacock who lives with a partner who plays the silent-treatment-game as a form of punishment. It is also the quickest way to drive them out and away to seek company elsewhere.

The term, 'over the top' was invented for Peacocks. If a little bit is good, then a lot must be better. Whether they are using ointment, shampoo, toothpaste or suntan lotion, the theme, 'Nothing Succeeds Like Excess,' is always playing in the background.

Not only do they wear their heart on their sleeve, they also wear their ills on their sleeve. When they are not feeling well, you will know about it — in fact the world will know about it! And in keeping with their sense of drama, if they have a cold it will be pneumonia, and if they have a headache it will be a migraine.

As children, they were bright, happy, talkative and cheeky. "Look Mum — I can ride no hands!" was a childhood theme that has tended to stay with them into adulthood. They generally either wrecked their toys or quickly became bored with them. This is another theme that has tended to stay with them — only their toys have become bigger and more expensive!

Also as kids, they could throw a temper tantrum worthy of an Academy Award. They were the sorts of kids who were into everything. If there was a dare going, they would be the ones to take it. And they would generally come out of it with skun knees, torn clothes and bruises. But totally undaunted and ready for the next dare!

With an extremely active imagination, coupled with their talkative nature and a total aversion to boredom, and with the natural skills of being creative and conceptual, rather than analytical, Peacocks don't normally do well in the school system. It is just not designed for them, nor does it cater for them. As a result, they are often branded as suffering from 'Attention Deficit Disorder' — or some other tag. This is rubbish of course. That just makes it easier for the teachers. If you can't understand it, then give it a name, get them out of the way and let's get on with teaching the 'normal' kids. As a result, Peacock children generally just scrape through school and can't wait 'to get the Hell outa there!' And you can hardly blame them.

Generous and friendly to a fault, Peacocks are extremely hospitable people. Visitors are always welcome in their homes. They also love spending time with children and are normally just as imaginative and playful as the kids they are with.

They are generally unstructured (they hate structure), disorganised, untidy, messy and invariably never on time. For those who live with a Peacock they know that it's pointless to expect meals at normal times, or for them to be ready to eat them at normal times. In fact they don't expect them to be on time for anything. What they do expect though, is that the Peacock will forget to set the alarm clock!

Smooth talkers, they take pride in being able to get their point across by being verbally persuasive. They also enjoy lively arguments and verbal jousting, which other personalities can see as either aggressive, or having a gift of the gab. They can also be very inventive with the truth. Prone to exaggeration, they never let the facts get in the way of a good story — or a good excuse that might get them out of a tight spot. They are the Kings and Queens of thinking on their feet.

With their vividly imaginative minds, Peacocks are forever thinking up great ideas that will make a fortune. The trouble is that they are far better at thinking than actually doing anything about them. Starting out with the best of intentions they normally run out of steam fairly quickly. I have a Peacock friend who has the nick-name 'Gunna' because he always says he's gunna do this, and gunna do that, but has never as far as I know, finished what he started. The song, *Seemed Like a Good Idea at the Time* was written for Peacocks.

Because Peacocks are so impulsive, they can also be compulsive. They can be compulsive gamblers, compulsive drinkers, and the like. *The song Can't help myself — bad habits* was also written for the Peacocks. Self-discipline is not big on their agenda of priorities. And because of their need for recognition, and to maintain the 'right image', they will often go recklessly into debt to 'look good'. Financial management is certainly not one of their strengths. As my Peacock friend says, "I never let poverty get in the way of a good time!"

Peacocks are rarely, if ever, self-critical or in the blame. They have a marvellous knack of being able to move the blame to others or to ' just bad luck' for any woes that may have befallen them, or for their own shortcomings.

When put out, the Peacock is the original 'dummy-spitter'. They are loud, dramatic, have a child-like temper and a sharp stinging tongue. But no sooner do they erupt like a volcano than within minutes they want to be friends again with all forgotten and forgiven. This sudden-eruption-to-fast-quiet-calm can have an extremely upsetting effect on a partner who may need a little more time to settle down. But it should be said that of all the personality styles, the Peacock is the least of the grudge-holders. They literally do forgive and forget. They are 'live and let live' people.

Peacocks are born lovers. Imaginative and impulsive (when they are interested, that is), they can be the most romantic, fascinating and creatively passionate love partners of all the personality styles. Expensive gifts, romantic words and generous gestures add to the excitement of a romance with the Peacock. But when they lose interest — that's it, full stop! When they feel the pinch of a collar or a short leash being applied, they can quickly hear the call to wander.

In a relationship, Peacocks are playmates rather than the soul mates. Impulsive and emotionally high strung, when things are going well for them, they can have very high highs, and when they're not — they can have very low lows. This can cause emotional static in a relationship, which can often be unstable because of it. Also because of their need for novelty, variety and change, long-term commitment is not one of their long suits. It's no coincidence that Hollywood is full of Peacocks with a high divorce rate. But if they are interested, they make passionate and committed mates.

Although not a big Pygmalion Game player, (they are after all, live-and-let-live people), never the less, the Peacock can attempt to chisel away at their mates with comments such as, "Come on, lighten up a bit." "You take life too seriously — have some fun." And by using their anthem: "You only live once, we're here for a good time — not a long time."

Interestingly enough, Peacocks are often drawn to Owl mates (opposites attract?). Perhaps the Peacock offers excitement and variety to the Owl, and the Owl offers structure and stability to the Peacock. Who knows?

In a nutshell, the Peacock is carefree, socially confident and outgoing; they have a strong social presence. They are talkative, energetic, optimistic, free-spirited, impulsive, enthusiastic, imaginative, witty, passionate, romantic, self-reliant, assertive, inventive, colourful and adaptable. They can also be disorganised, untidy, angry, emotional, persuasive, and manipulative — but always lovable — if you can stand the ups and downs!

Switch the TV on any night to see the Peacocks in action. They love being on the small screen — although being on the big one is better!

Some of the Peacocks you may be able to relate to are: Gary Sweet, Sam Newman, Sarah Ferguson, Jack Nicholson, Jim Carrey, Paul Hogan, Libbi Gorr (Elle McFeast), Rex Hunt, Cher, Eddie Murphy, Wendy Harmer, Graham Richardson, Steve Martin, Oprah Winfrey, Barry Humphries' Edna Everage character, Pamela Anderson Lee, Barry Humphries' Les Patterson character, H G Nelson, Shane Warne, John McEnroe, Lleyton Hewitt, Alan Bond, Jacques Villeneuve, Kylie Minogue, Danni Minogue, Ronald Reagan, Mel Gibson, Naomi Campell, Cindy Crawford, Charlie Sheen, Mikey Robbins, Billy Connolly, James

Bond, anyone on the 'Big Brother' show — and the ultimate Peacock, Miss Piggy from the Muppets!

Strength and Weakness

How can some people see the Peacock as outgoing, talkative, energetic and flamboyant, while others may see them as superficial, self-indulgent, loud and a show-off?

The answer lies in our inherent strengths and weaknesses, which is a double-edged sword. And it can cut both ways. Simply put, our weaknesses are our strengths that we have taken too far.

When the Peacock is working on his or her strengths they appear outgoing, talkative, energetic and flamboyant. But if they take these strengths too far, they can be seen as superficial, self-indulgent, loud and a show-off. But of course it all depends on who is looking at the time. We will talk more about this later.

"We're put on this earth to help each other."

The Anthem of the Dove

MEET THE DOVE

The Dove

Described by some as kind, gentle, shy, friendly and sincere, and by others as gullible, over-sensitive and wimpy, the Dove is driven by the need for acceptance, love, friendship and belonging. They just can't get enough of it.

They are socially reserved, friendly and can be quite shy with strangers. They are unassuming, courteous and well mannered. They talk softly and are quiet and gentle people. They are the 'gentle-ladies' and 'gentle-men' of the world.

Slower paced, easygoing and relaxed, they listen with interest and watch people's faces intently as they listen. They respond with attentive smiles and nods, their facial expressions reflecting and reacting to what is being said, and they will often spontaneously touch the person they are speaking to.

Doves are the peaceful people of the world. Patient and tolerant, they generally look for, and see, the good in people. They will do almost anything to avoid dealing with difficult people or conflict situations. As mentioned before, their driving need is for *acceptance, love, friendship and belonging*. Because of this, they will avoid upsetting or offending anyone at all costs, which can sometimes be to the detriment of their own well-being and happiness. 'Peace at any price' is the Dove's anthem.

Understated like themselves, their cars are normally modest, rarely gaudy in colour, and may well have stickers on the back window. These can be of a fish, or 'Baby on Board', or 'Save the Whale', (they are big on saving things, especially animals and the environment).

Friendly and pleasant to be with, Doves are extremely caring and supportive. They are good listeners who always have a willing and sympathetic ear for any problems that might be ailing you. Doves are the people that other people tell their secrets to.

Doves are the most gentle and caring of all the personality styles. And they are blessed (or cursed?) with a strong conscience and often try too hard to 'do the right thing' and to please others. They have a fear of hurting anyone's feelings; they are natural diplomats and peacemakers and will always try and settle disputes with caring and kindness.

They are not particularly concerned with achievement, possessions or material things. Rather, their goal in life is to have harmony and happiness. It was probably a Dove who coined the saying "Money doesn't buy you happiness."

Inhibited, self-conscious and wanting to be unobtrusive, one of their fears is to be embarrassed in any way. One of their greatest anxieties is to be made the centre of attention — to be pushed into the public spotlight. If this happens, the Dove becomes confused and embarrassed to the point of literally being lost for words and will blush with painful intensity. This is the main reason why there are so few examples of Doves in the public eye. Those who have been, or are in the public eye, have invariably been forced into that position.

Doves could not be called risk-takers or adventurers. They generally take a hesitant and rather timid approach to life. They like to deal with familiar situations and people. They tend to stay in the same place, whether it be a home, (which always looks and feels 'homely') or a job. They are uncomfortable with any changes or disruptions to their normal way of doing things. Because of this, they are good at doing jobs in an accepted and predictable pattern, and often find work where those qualities are called for.

Because they are natural co-operators and 'people-centred', with great compassion and empathic skills, they often find careers (although it's more like a calling rather than a profession for the Dove), as social workers, psychologists, counsellors, nurses, teachers, receptionists, doctors, volunteers, waiters, zoo keepers, red cross workers, missionary workers, and the like. Also, some of the most famous poets and romantic novelists, today and throughout history have been Doves.

Patient and tolerant, placid and peaceful, they make warm and loving partners. Shy in a large group, they prefer the company of people they are familiar with and close to. To these people they are the most loving, reliable and loyal of friends. Although shy, quiet and retiring in public, with friends and family they can talk the leg off a chair. In a comfortable familiar situation they are the chatterers of the world!

They love to 'people watch' and 'read people' for their personalities. And they love reading books like this one!

Besides their family and close friends, one of their greatest loves is listening to music. Sentimental and romantic, they cry easily in sad films. They will tend to keep any tokens of love or friendship that you give them, and they are big on keeping well-categorised photo albums, sometimes with little comments written on sticky labels stuck under each photograph.

As children, the Doves were the quiet, sensitive kids. They were never deceitful or cunning. If they were ever punished, especially if wrongfully, they would be deeply offended and hurt by the injustice of it. And they could be just as hurt seeing other kids punished, whether they deserved it or not.

Doves quickly discovered that the strategy of withdrawing and going quiet was a great way to 'disappear' and keep out of trouble. And this strategy has seemed to serve them well for the rest of their lives. In the playground they would hang back until invited by the other kids to join in the group or game; if not asked, they would play by themselves secretly yearning to be involved but too shy to push themselves in.

Dove children often felt different from the other kids and didn't know why — a feeling many of them still feel as adults.

In the classroom, they were seen by the teacher as the 'perfect student and child', because they were so 'quiet and well-mannered — no trouble at all'. In other words, they made the teacher's job that much easier. Although eager to learn and wanting to do well at school, unfortunately because of their quiet and placid nature, rather than ask questions when confused (which they very often were and still are), they would sit back quietly and fall behind in the lesson. As a result, they would generally just scrape through the exams and yearn for the day when they could leave.

After leaving school Doves can well become 'intellectual butterflies'. Rather than concentrating and perhaps specialising deeply in one field or area of knowledge (as the Owl would do), they tend to flit from one thing to another. Much of their reading is often in the area of personal enlightenment, self-development, spiritual-type philosophies (especially Eastern philosophies) and the pursuit of 'wholeness as a person'.

The 'search for self' — the pursuit of 'self as a whole person' — finding the 'real self,' can often be a life-long project for a Dove. They tend to be constantly self examining themselves and their lives. Many Doves often live with the nagging feeling that perhaps they are not 'quite whole', that perhaps there is more to it. The song, *Is That All There Is?* was written for the Dove.

For many Doves, their personal journey, their 'search for self', often ends by simply forgiving themselves for their human frailties and accepting themselves for who they are — warts and all. The journey ends with unconditional self-love and total self-acceptance and the realisation that 'you can't truly love another until you first love yourself'. When this happens, it can be a time of exhilarating peace and freedom for the Dove.

Doves can also be incredibly intuitive. They can 'pick up vibes' as the old saying goes. They know instinctively what other people are thinking, sometimes to the point of being able to actually read another person's mind. Or they can walk into an empty room and know that there has been an argument there only minutes before. Most of the legitimate psychics and mystics are Doves.

Because Doves are so sensitive (hypersensitive) and empathetic, they can tend to 'over-empathise'. It's as if they can actually feel the emotional experiences of others. In a sickroom, for instance, where others are suffering, they can get so emotionally involved and empathic that they become distressed to the point of giddiness, even actually fainting. In fearful or critical situations, Doves can become confused and immobilised (they freeze). Their emotional circuits seem to overload and short out, especially when it comes to an emotional experience of conflict and hurt.

Doves are idealists. They are the romantics. And they can more often than not have an ideal view of love — a romantic fantasy or storybook idea of love — a belief that 'love will conquer all'. Some Doves can be inclined to search for the 'perfect love' going from one relationship to another, but because in the world of reality there is no perfect person, no perfect love, no ideal, they can often become disillusioned. They can tend to project their own romantic ideals onto loved ones who never quite measure up. So, for many Doves, falling in love (being in love with love) can be happier than the actual reality of loving.

Of all the personality styles, Doves are the most prone to feelings of jealousy, and while they can be most forgiving of others, they tend to be tentative in their own self-esteem, and can be quite harsh and critical of themselves. Because of this, they respond warmly to encouragement, praise and compliments, which if in a relationship with an Eagle or an Owl, can come few and far between.

Because of their strong empathy and will to please, coupled with a sometimes frail sense of self, in a relationship they can make their loved ones the 'centre of their world' and tend to identify so strongly with their partner that they'll often adopt their partner's opinions and view of life as their own. Having said that, although tranquil, considerate and easygoing, deep down the Dove is full of enthusiasm, causes, fierce loyalties and

strong opinions, although they seldom talk about these things unless they know you well. But make no mistake, once committed to an idea, a belief, a person, or an opinion, the Dove can be obstinate and single-minded in their beliefs, stubborn and immovable.

On a similar note; as much as the Dove strives for harmony in their relationships, when in a relationship with an Eagle they have an instinctive and reflexive reaction to invariably disagree with them. If the Eagle says it's black, the Dove says it's dark grey. If the Eagle says it's hot, the Dove says it's only warm. As an Eagle always thinks that he or she is always right, this constant 'correction' can drive them nuts!

Interestingly enough, Doves are often attracted to eagles and vice versa. (Opposites attract?). Perhaps the Dove offers the Eagle compassion, sensitivity and caring, and the Eagle offers the Dove decisiveness, strength and protection — making up a yin and yang relationship. Who knows? But whatever it is, these relationships have a long and happy history of success.

Quiet, placid and 'peace at any price' people, it is against everything they stand for to express their negative feelings in personal confrontation — they would rather act the peacemaker. But the downside of this is that differences never expressed never become resolved. Also, if the Dove is put under stress, or if they are forced to do something they don't agree with, they can do a 'slow burn' and play the 'quiet withdrawal game'. Because of their passive nature, the 'silent treatment,' (or the 'Martyr Game') works well for them because it can cause the issue to be raised by their partner without them seeming to initiate it.

In a relationship they often play the part of their partner's 'conscience-keeper,' and can tend to use this as chisels for their Pygmalion Games. But having said that, Doves have the greatest natural gifts of all the styles for happy relationships. Placid-tempered, affectionate and kind natured, Doves are 'soul mates'. They offer tranquil, comfortable stability.

With their natural inclination to want to please and not make waves, Doves can be very susceptible to being 'carved' by the Pygmalion chisels of a more assertive partner to the point of becoming, and conforming, to the sort of person their partner wants them to be, and consequently if they are not careful, can lose much of their individual identity in the process.

Peaceful, loving and tender, they are the least 'moody' of all the personality styles, and one of the most loyal and pleasant to live with. In a relationship with the Dove you rarely have to 'test the wind' to find out what mood they're in. Like almost everything else about them, they are comfortably and pleasantly predictable. They provide anchorage and a safe harbour for those with less predictable personality styles.

Some of the Doves you may be able to relate to are: Robin Williams, (who often plays 'Dove roles'), Hazel Hawke, the late Princess Diana, the characters invariably played by the actor Hugh Grant, Olivia Newton John, George Harrison (The Beatles), Tiger Woods, Pat Rafter, the Dalai Lama, and the character played by the child actor Haley Joel Osmet in the movie *The Sixth Sense*.

Strength and Weakness

How can some people see the Dove as kind, gentle, shy, friendly and sincere, while others may see them as gullible, over-sensitive and wimpy?

The answer lies in our inherent strengths and weaknesses, which is a double-edged sword. And it can cut both ways. Simply put, our weaknesses are our strengths that we have taken too far.

When the Dove is working on his or her strengths they appear kind, gentle, shy, friendly and sincere. But if they take these strengths too far, they can be seen as gullible, over-sensitive and wimpy. But of course it all depends on who is looking at the time. We will talk more about this later.

"Coming second means you're the first of the losers."

The Anthem of the Eagle

The Eagle

MEET THE EAGLE

Described by some as independent, confident, assertive, bold and decisive, and by others as aggressive, bossy, rude and arrogant, the Eagle is driven by the need for control, authority and power. They love it. They just can't get enough of it.

Eagles are socially self-assured and quick in both the way they talk and the way they move. They tend to convey a forceful, no nonsense air of importance about them.

They use little facial expression and show hardly, if any, emotion. They give the impression of being in total control of themselves and the situation at all times, which they generally are.

Often described as having piercing eyes, they will look you straight in the eye. When they talk there is little, if any, preceding small talk, or 'verbal foreplay'. They get straight down to business — right to the bottom line.

The Eagle is unconcerned with fashion. They normally dress well but conservatively, in sober colours, neither fashionable nor unfashionable. The way they dress could be described as efficient and practical. In other words, you rarely notice what they are wearing.

Generally of good spirits, they are hearty, frank and forthright people. While socially confident and often quite charming, they can convey the impression of being uncomfortable with socialising and small talk. They look as if they would rather be somewhere else that's more important. And make no mistake; this is not just an impression. To the Eagle, play is work and work is play. In fact, much of their socialising invariably combines a work element.

But don't be fooled, eagles have a keen sense of humour and a great sense of fun. It's just that they hate to waste their time on what they see as useless socialising. If there is no 'payoff' in the socialising, then it becomes work. And when forced to do it, they can appear a bit removed and above it all.

Their form of relaxation and recreation will invariably involve some form of risk-taking, competitiveness or skill, or all three combined. Or it can just as well take the form of intellectual pursuits — the acquiring of knowledge, as in reading, studying and the like. And they are apt to turn to one new interest after another. They enjoy adding to their fund of knowledge and take a great deal of pride in what they know. Much of their self-respect comes from their grasp of intellectual principles and knowledge of their field of expertise.

Persuasive, articulate and normally well informed, they are skilful in finding logical reasons for what they want and are good at getting others to go along with them. These skills also make them competent public speakers and sharp negotiators.

Proudly independent thinkers, they place great value on having personal freedom, and pride themselves on living by their own rules. They are innovators, initiators and self-starters who generally act while others are still thinking about it. Quick and decisive, they hate not being in control of things — themselves, the situation, and those around them. As mentioned before, they are *driven by the need for control, authority and power*.

Dominant, fast paced, and assertive, they do everything with a sense of urgency. They are the controllers and commanders of the world. And they can appear quite intimidating to some of the less assertive personality styles.

Ambitious and self-assured, they tend to seek positions of authority, responsibility and power ("without power you can't get things done or change anything"). They are attracted to jobs where they can use their intellectual and strategic skills to bring about change and get results. Cool-headed and strong in a crisis situation, they can quickly sum up a situation, take charge, bring about the required action, and generally resolve it. They are good people to have in a tight spot and on your side. But not so good to have on the other side!

As children, they were the kids described as 'bright and alert'. They were intellectually clever in the classroom and seemed to breeze through school without too much effort. They passed their exams with high marks without too much study, while the rest of the class slogged it out for an average score. As kids, they were smart and knew it, and still do. They were generally popular with both their fellow students and the teachers alike. Although their teachers may have noted in their school reports, "This student can be a little headstrong."

They play to win. Bossy and imbued from birth with the 'killer instinct', in the playground, and later on the sports field, they wanted things to go their way. Fiercely competitive, it didn't matter if it was hopscotch or tennis — they had to win — and they generally did! To the Eagle there is no second prize. As an Eagle friend of mine says, "Coming second means you're the first of the losers." To the Eagle, "Winning isn't everything — it's the only thing."

Eagles are pragmatists. They take the shortest and quickest path or approach to getting where they want to be. They are not much on abstract theories, or learning for the sake of learning (which is an Owl trait). Eagles listen and learn for what they can use. ("If you can't use it, eat it, or have sex with it, then what's the use of it?"). Sceptical by nature, if they can't feel it, touch it, or see it, it doesn't exist. And, "If it doesn't exist — then what's the point of it?"

Harsh and critical to human foibles of any description, they can be scornful and severe, and convey an air of arrogant indifference to us 'lesser mortals'.

When put out the Eagle can attack viciously and with venom. They can seethe with outrage when they feel an injustice has been done to them. And they are quick to seek revenge against their foes. Strong willed and determined, once they have closed the door on an enemy — that's it — finished!

Determined and self-reliant risk-takers, many of our adventurers and explorers throughout history were Eagles — as were many of our early pioneers. (The Doves and Owls came later as settlers).

Enthusiastic, courageous and intelligent, others seem to naturally look to them for leadership. Like their bird counterpart, they have long-range vision and totally focus on their goals. And once their mind is made up they are absolutely unstoppable. They invariably get what they set out for.

They like to have the final say in everything. They give the orders. They delegate. And they will not wait — for anything. They have a 'Waiting-Patience-Level' of zero!

They rarely, if ever, doubt that their opinions or judgements might be wrong. They convey a 'born-to-rule-and-do-it-my-way' commanding feel about them. Interestingly enough, most people seem to do just what Eagles tell them to do. This born-to-rule attitude can often be seen by some of the less assertive personality styles as conceit and arrogance. (As an Eagle friend of mine once said to me when challenged on this, "When does 'confidence' become 'arrogance'? I suppose it depends on who's looking at the time — and anyway, who cares?")

The character of General Patton played by George C. Scott in the movie, *Patton* is a classic portrayal of the Eagle — a cool, tough, unemotional character who gets the job done without any sentiment getting in the way.

Confident, strong, decisive, self-reliant and goal-centred, Eagles are natural leaders, and have been throughout history — Napoleon, General Douglas Macarthur of the USA, General John Monash of Australia, Margaret Thatcher of Britain, Saddam Hussein of Iran, Chairman Mao of China, Fidel Castro of Cuba, Lee Kwan Yew of Singapore, Dr Mahatir Mohamad of Malaysia — Eagles all.

Eagles are the workaholics of the world. They never knock off. They can get so absorbed in, and so preoccupied with their work that they become totally oblivious to the 'little people things' that may be happening around them. And if they are not careful, this can affect their personal relationships.

When they talk they don't waste words. With a sharp intelligent mind hidden behind a somewhat expressionless face, coupled with an intellectual need to be precise and to the point, they often appear impatient and abrupt, especially to Doves. What many people don't realise is that they think and talk in 'bullet points', their thinking is normally five beats ahead of whoever is talking to them. Because of this, they get annoyed at having to give drawn out explanations — or having to hear them. They try to avoid the irrelevant and the trivial. They believe that what they see as obvious to them should be obvious to everyone else. And they will (often rudely) interrupt others when they are talking to get their point across.

Thinkers rather than feelers, intellectual rather than emotional, they have little patience and low tolerance for any display of feelings or emotions. And they get very impatient with 'emotional reasoning', unsupported facts, or 'flaky logic'. They will never be persuaded by what they see as an 'inferior argument'. Nor do they have much patience for people who are evasive or beat around the bush. Eagles are rational, logical, straight-to-the-point people — and they wish that you were too!

One of their biggest hates is hearing excuses, especially long rambling ones. And sometimes you will hear them say under their breath, between gritted teeth; "God must have loved stupid people, he made so many of them!" When you ask them a question, you will always get a short answer — quick and to the point — no messing around. And unless you ask for more explanation, that is all you'll get, end of story.

They secretly take great pride in their sharp intellectual ability, (which they actually have in aces). But this can sometimes appear to others as arrogance — a look-down-the-nose attitude of intellectual superiority and can quite unconsciously adopt an almost 'parent-teacher' attitude. This can happen when the Eagle expounds on a subject while assuming their listener has no knowledge of it, irrespective of whether they do or not.

Their impatience and inability to stop, slow down and listen to the thoughts and opinions of others, especially about 'people things' can be frustrating and off-putting. Unfortunately for the Eagle, most human beings are — well, human beings, and are more emotional than logical. Most of us do not have their sharp, quick rational mind, nor do we have their natural ability to discuss a subject in a quick analytical and succinct way. When it comes to sitting down and 'simply talking', especially about relationships, being quick and analytical are perhaps the least important skills needed.

Eagles are not big into giving compliments. They are extremely uncomfortable and embarrassed when it comes to praising others. They don't expect it and wonder why the Hell others want it. (Interestingly enough, many Eagles don't expect to be liked — leave alone praised). If they do praise, it will normally be given for what the person did, not for who they are.

If you happen to praise an Eagle, be careful. First you will probably embarrass them, and secondly, being the mistrusting sceptics they are, they'll wonder what you want!

Although they are 'hard taskmasters' and 'mistresses', they are nowhere near as hard on others as they are on themselves. Deep down, Eagles are constantly criticising and disparaging themselves for their flaws and frailties. They hold themselves strictly accountable. But having said that, it should be added that they are hardly (if ever) unsure of themselves and their abilities.

Because they control and hide their feelings as much as possible, some see them as cold and stiff. Although opening up their hearts and sharing their feelings is foreign to their nature, this seemingly 'arrogant self-control' is the source of much misunderstanding in their relationships. But make no mistake — Eagles are people of mighty passion. They have a hard shell and a soft centre. They need plenty of love because, as those who live with them know, deep down they are the most sensitive of creatures.

Eagles make strong, loving and protective mates and parents. They provide a family with a solid sense of security. The paradox (and we all have them), in the Eagle's nature is that while they want to go out and conquer the world, they also want their personal lives, and their personal relationships, to have predictable and comfortable patterns. They want their home life to be quiet, settled, tranquil and organised. They want comfortable stability.

Their main Pygmalion Game is to become bossy, using the chisels of impatience, criticism, facts, logic, or sarcasm, or all of them at once to the point of becoming overbearing when their loved ones do not live up to their high expectations. But having said that, Eagles are generally the least active of all the Pygmalion chisellers. They are generally non-manipulative and rarely, if ever, try to punish their loved ones, and they never punish them emotionally. Because they place so much value on their own personal freedom of action, they firmly believe that their mates should also have the same freedom to develop in their own direction, and they seldom step in to interfere.

Because of their need to control and their commanding presence, there are many Eagles in the public eye. They can be seen in politics, leaders of unions and businesses. Some prominent Australian Eagles include Kerry Packer, Rupert Murdoch, Bronwyn Bishop, Jenny George (Past ACTU President), Jeff Kennett, Pauline Hanson, Simon Crean, Greg Norman, Germaine Greer, Peter Reith, Amanda Vanstone, Lisa Curry-Kenny, Steve Waugh. Others include; Judge Judy (Judy Sheindlin), Hilary Clinton, and almost any part played by Arnold Schwarzenegger, Bruce Willis, or Clint Eastwood.

Also, if you haven't already seen it, hire and watch the movie "Heat" with Robert De Niro and Al Pacino. They both play Eagles operating on opposite sides of the law. The scene where they both meet for coffee in the diner 'for a chat' (Eagles don't chat!) is worth the price of hiring it. The movie finishes tragically, but right to the end, both respect each other. Respect is the greatest compliment you can pay an Eagle. They don't much care whether or not you like them, but they care a great deal about whether or not you respect them.

Strength and Weakness

How can some people see the Eagle as independent, confident, assertive, bold and decisive, while others may see them as aggressive, bossy, rude and arrogant?

The answer lies in our inherent strengths and weaknesses, which is a double-edged sword. And it can cut both ways. Simply put, our weaknesses are our strengths that we have taken too far.

When the Eagle is working on his or her strengths they appear independent, confident, assertive, bold and decisive. But if they take these strengths too far, they can be seen as aggressive, bossy, rude and arrogant. But of course it all depends on who is looking at the time. We will talk more about this later.

*"Fools rush in where
wise men fear
to tread."*

The Anthem of the Owl

The Owl

MEET THE OWL

Described by some as conservative, quiet, gentle, dignified and well mannered, and by others as fussy, cool, withdrawn, and a stick in the mud, the Owl is driven by the need for certainty and predictability. They just can't get enough of it.

Owls are socially reserved, quiet, and formal and can give the impression of being somewhat cool, withdrawn, serious and distant.

They use little facial expression or body language. They are the least (outwardly) emotionally expressive of all the personality styles.

Owls are distant, thoughtful and introspective. Socially, they can give you the impression they would rather be doing something else. Which is exactly what they are thinking! Socialising is not one of their preferred activities and it can be quite uncomfortable for them. To be honest, they would much rather be doing something more useful.

They invariably wear beards; the men that is! But both male and female Owls tend to wear conservative sober colours, especially brown, beige and other earthy colours. They have little concern with fashion or style and are not preoccupied with 'what goes with what'. They are conservative in every respect. The female Owl wears 'serious and sensible' clothes with a hairstyle to match. They wear little, if any, jewellery or other 'fancy adornments', (their words). And they will wear their clothes until they are well worn. Owls try to get the last drop out of almost everything.

Sober, serious and analytical, Owls are the perfectionists and traditionalists of the world and are often described as 'solid citizens' — the 'pillars of society' — 'the salt-of-the-earth'. They always conduct themselves with a sense of decency and decorum.

Owls are often described as 'Victorian' (as in the era of Queen Victoria), when adherence to decency, dignity ('keeping a stiff upper lip') orderliness, discipline, industriousness, obedience, modesty and a belief in traditional authority was the order of the day. They observe standards of conduct religiously. Today, many of these values are seen as straight laced and prim and proper. But it is the steadfast Owls amongst us who provide the foundation to our communities and provide the glue which holds our societies together.

Upholders of traditional values, rituals and social ceremonies, they have great respect for rules, accepted procedures, and especially for law and order. To the Owl, rules are important and should be adhered to. Because of this they often find careers and jobs as the guardians of law and order. 'Correctness in all things' is a theme that runs throughout the Owl's life. They are concerned with how they are viewed by society and especially with what the neighbours may think. Their reputation as a sensible and responsible law-abiding member of their community is guarded with a fierce determination. In the Owl's world there is right and wrong, black and white, and many shoulds and shouldn'ts.

Owls are independent and private people. They keep themselves to themselves. They value their privacy and solitude and are more than happy to be alone. They enjoy their own company and tend to get upset if visitors 'pop in' unannounced.

As children they were well mannered, respectful and responsible. They were often described by adults as being 'good sensible kids', and as 'having an old head on young shoulders'. They looked after their toys, (they may still have some in mint condition), and always put them back where they belonged after playing with them. At school they were studious and conscientious students who kept their nose to the grindstone and invariably did well in their exams.

Because Owls are logical, organised, accurate and precise, they will often find careers as: bankers, lawyers, judges, librarians, editors, secretaries, accountants, quality controllers, auditors, surgeons, dentists — careers that require their analytical, structured and methodical mind — and where they can generally work alone as Owls are solitary people. In these types of jobs they are square pegs in square holes, and like everything else in life, they take it very seriously and will stay in the same job, at the same place, for long lengths of time. They are the people who stay around long enough to get long service leave and collect twenty-five years of superannuation payments.

Their work place is usually efficient and business-like, unadorned with pictures or any other 'superfluous adornments'. (It may even look like an operating theatre!) And it is rarely, if ever, rearranged.

Far from being the wittiest or humorous of people ("Life is too serious to be frivolous, and I'm no good at telling jokes, anyway.") never the less, they can have a very dry and often sardonic sense of humour.

The Owl is practical, logical, analytical and factual.

They become extremely uncomfortable and a closed book when it comes to the subject of emotions or discussing emotional issues. They tend to think in straight lines and believe that thinking is more important than feeling. They are embarrassed by any displays of emotion and think people should keep their feelings under control and to themselves. Even those who live with Owls admit that they are hard to get to know at an emotional level.

Another way of masking their emotions, both to themselves and to others, or to escape from an emotional situation rather than have to handle it, is to become absorbed in some form of work-like activity, particularly something which involves them in details.

Owls are strictly practical thinkers. If they cannot feel, see or touch it, then it doesn't exist. Because of this, they have little, if any, intuitive ability — the ability to see the unseen. For example, during a conversation where another personality style may quickly pick up on all the 'vibes' and unspoken messages that are being sent, the Owl can be quite oblivious to them. In fact, they may even argue that such a thing does not exist. As over eighty per cent of how we communicate is conveyed by what is *not* said, this can be a real challenge when it comes to having a relationship with an Owl. The term, "Oh, you know what I mean..." makes no sense at all to them. They do not know what you mean. When you ask an Owl to 'read between the lines,' all they see are the blank spaces!

Serious and quiet, they earn success by concentration and thoroughness. Practical, orderly, matter of fact, logical, realistic and dependable, they see to it that everybody is well organised. They take responsibility. They make up their own minds as to what should be accomplished and work toward it steadily, regardless of distractions.

They are especially punctual people and tend to get annoyed when others are not as strict at observing the same courtesy. An Owl business friend of mine has a saying, "If you can't be on time — be early." That says it all when it comes to the Owl in relation to punctuality and they can be very critical and impatient with Peacocks (who see time as elastic!). Owls view this as self-indulgent and a total lack of discipline. (Discipline is high on their list of priorities and they abhor self-indulgence).

Owls are self-disciplined people and they can have quite a puritan and moralistic attitude to those who aren't. They rarely drink to excess (that's if they drink at all), never smoke, and see themselves as having few, if any, bad habits, and are usually quite critical and intolerant of those who do. An Owl friend of mine believes that sex is something you only do in the bedroom, and always with the light off!

They are definitely not the risk takers of the world. Almost every word, thought and action is driven by the Owl's major motivating *need for certainty and predictability*, in a word, *stability*. They abhor the unexpected and are generally most uncomfortable with change. They do not like having their routine disturbed in any way. They want their life to follow a set, predictable and comfortable pattern.

The world can be a scary and distrustful place for the Owl. 'Trust no one' could well be their anthem. They are the biggest buyers of locks, security products, insurance and Volvo cars! Before buying something they will do exhaustive research, collecting and studying any literature on it that they can get their hands on. They are always looking for statistics, evidence, facts — proof. They just can't get enough information. They need to be right. They need to be certain.

Prone to being pessimistic and cynical ("What if...?"), they believe wholeheartedly in Murphy's Law; 'Whatever will go wrong will go wrong'. (There are some Owls who think Murphy was an optimist!) This sceptical outlook can make them quite suspicious and always looking for 'the catch'. They want to see the written guarantees and tend to buy only the tried and proven — the safest.

Because of their need for certainty, it can make them quite indecisive. They will often use the saying, 'Fools rush in where wise men fear to tread', as a justification for much of their over-cautiousness and indecision.

When they are talking, even socially, everything must be accurate and precise, often to the point of frustration for their listener: "I was talking to John the other day, no hang on, it wasn't John, it was Graham, or was it Brad..." And something won't be "around $10.00," it will be "$9.93," or whatever the correct and actual price or decimal place is. (Remember, they need to be right). If you want to talk about something that interests them, no matter what you ask, they will give you 'the long answer', whether you wanted it or not. It has been said that when you ask an Owl the time they will tell you how a clock works!

With observant eyes and ears always at the ready, they are always up with the latest goings on. Little slips past them. They are invariably a great source for getting the latest gossip, and are usually keen to let you know about it!

Owls can be very frugal with their money, or as the saying goes, "They give a dollar a good home." Big spenders they are not. At a restaurant they will calculate and split shared bills to the cent. To other personality styles this carefulness with money is often seen as 'mean and stingy' rather than 'careful'. Because of their frugality and their cautiousness, there are not too many of them who are members of Gamblers Anonymous. In fact, the idea of gambling, or why somebody would want to do it, is totally beyond them. ("It's too hard to get without giving it away.")

No matter how much money the Owl may have, because of their careful nature and need for security, they are usually good savers who have adequate reserves. Yet they never seem to have enough. (How much security is enough?) When discussing money matters they will invariably 'talk poor'.

The Owl is structured and systemised in everything they do. They stick to a set routine. Neat and tidy in their habits, (they tend to tidy incessantly), there is a place for everything and everything is in its place. And it annoys them when others put things out of place. They keep a well-organised diary and write 'to do' lists for everything. They always read the instructions and fine print before using a new appliance. And they are the people that Peacocks ask to program their VCRs for them!

Over-cautious, they are incessant double-checkers, always checking locked doors (at least twice) to make doubly sure they are locked.

Owls are not in the habit of opening their hearts, nor could they be called 'the romantics of life'. They become exhausted coping with too much emotion. Of all the styles, the Owl is the most susceptible to emotional overload. But make no mistake; they have strong feelings that they keep well hidden and guarded. Giving in to their emotions is seen as rather weak and self-indulgent. But they feel their emotions just as intensely as any of the other styles; they just do not express them — especially when hurt. Rather than getting it off their chest, they tend to suffer in silence, become depressed, and seek the solitude of their own company. When this happens, their partner can often feel shut out.

Intolerant, critical and disdainful of human frailties and foibles, if the Owl is not careful, they can give the impression of conveying a rather superior and puritan attitude. This can appear quite supercilious and 'holier than thou' to those who are not so moralistic.

Life is a serious business for the Owl — responsible, dutiful, steady, industrious, devoted, trustworthy, disciplined. They are a Rock of Gibraltar. And they often feel the weight of this responsibility bearing down on them. It's often in their nature to complain about being overworked, and although they sometimes seem to enjoy and take pride in how overworked they are, they may be haunted with a feeling of doom and gloom, plagued with a nagging feeling that they are somehow not quite living up to their duties and responsibilities (the greatest shame and humiliation for an Owl). As a result, they can become 'always tired', suffer headaches, chronic exhaustion and become depressive, especially suffering 'dawn depression'. Research seems to indicate that also added to these woes, Owls can suffer from back pain, stomach pains, ulcers and especially constipation — the typical 'up-tight' maladies.

Acting on emotions rather than on proven facts, goes totally against their grain. With a rather old-fashioned and traditional nature, Owls are as meticulous in the home as they are anywhere else; in fact they tend to be more so.

In a partnership with an Owl it is important to remember that they value their solitude and at times just want to be left alone. Although they can sometimes appear distant and aloof, the Owl has a deep internal world and cares deeply about their loved ones (in fact they can be quite possessive). Sober, reserved, careful, practical, orderly, dependable, reliable and loyal, the Owl is a stable and steady beacon in any relationship.

Owls are the nest-keepers. They have a parental instinct. And they like things to be settled and organised. Home is a place where there is order and rules, rituals and comfortable routines to follow with a dependable and faithful companion.

The Owl regards protecting and providing for the family, (conscientious devotion), as the deepest expression of their love. For the female Owl it may be the focal point of her life. Her devotion to her partner and children, preparing meals and keeping a clean and orderly house may take up all her time and become her reason for living. To some of the other personality types (and they are often drawn to Peacock mates), this can be seen as mind-numbing and deadly monotony. But as a matter of interest it should be noted that Owls stay married longer than any of the other types.

While the Owl seeks stability and hates family strife and division, if put under pressure, they can either withdraw within themselves and become quieter than normal, or just as easily become intolerant and critical, adopting the attitude of a stern parent and attempt to impose their own rather puritanical values ("You should be more responsible") onto their partner. In other words, their Pygmalion chisels can either be 'the silent treatment,' or nagging criticism which chips away at their mates.

Because of their need for privacy and the pursuits they involve themselves in, Owls are invariably 'back room' people, therefore it's hard coming up with names of public figures to give as examples, but some prominent Owls you may be able to relate to are: John Howard, Prince Charles and Woody Allen.

The character played by Anthony Hopkins in the British movie *Remains of the Day* is a classic portrayal of the Owl personality. Anthony Hopkins often plays an Owl personality and plays it to perfection (it's no coincidence, he himself is an Owl). See him also portray a typical Owl personality in the movie *Shadowlands*.

Strength and Weakness

How can some people see the Owl as conservative, quiet, gentle, dignified and well mannered, while others may see them as fussy, cool, withdrawn, and a stick in the mud?

The answer lies in our inherent strengths and weaknesses, which is a double-edged sword. And it can cut both ways. Simply put, our weaknesses are our strengths that we have taken too far.

When the Owl is working on his or her strengths they appear conservative, quiet, gentle, dignified and well mannered. But if they take these strengths too far, they can be seen as fussy, cool, withdrawn, and a stick in the mud. But of course it all depends on who is looking at the time. We'll talk more about this later.

PUBLIC FACES

DRIVING FORCES

**Emotionally-based
Imaginative and intuitive**

Driving
Force:
Recognition
Praise
Applause

The Peacock

The Dove

Driving
Force:
Love
Friendship
Belonging

Driving
Force:
Control
Authority
Power

The Eagle

The Owl

Driving
Force:
Certainty
Predictability
Stability

**Intellectually-based
Rational and analytical**

7

WHAT IS THIS THING CALLED LOVE?

When my wife and I were younger, before I knew about this personality stuff, I remember the Peacock in me said to her one day:

"You don't love me because you never tell me." (Peacock's are terribly insecure; we like to be told we are loved at least twice a day, if not more!). To which Val answered in her inimitable Dove way:

"I show you that I love you every day. I show you by what I do. I show you my love by action, not words."

And she was right. Doves show their love by supporting and caring.

Each style has its own kind of love.

We each define what love is through the 'perception-filters' of our personality style.

Ask a Peacock what love is.

Ask a Peacock what love is and they will tell you (you won't be able to stop them!) that love is telling your partner often that you love him or her, it's about praising them and complimenting them, telling them how terrific they are. In other words, all the things that the Peacock values.

Ask an Eagle what love is.

Ask an eagle what love is and they will tell you (with the help of a crowbar and truth serum!) that love is protecting and providing for the one you love, it's about respecting each other and allowing each other the freedom to grow within the relationship. In other words, all the things that the Eagle values.

Ask an Owl what love is.

Ask an Owl what love is and they will tell you (after you loosen them up a bit with a few red wines!) that love is being a guardian to the one you love, it's about providing for their comfort and giving them a safe, predictable and structured environment in which to live. In other words, all the things that the Owl values.

Ask a Dove what love is.

Ask a Dove what love is and they will tell you (without too much prompting) that love is caring for and supporting your loved one through thick and thin, it's about helping each other and being sensitive to each other's needs. In other words, all the things that the Dove values.

Love, like everything else, is different strokes for different folks.

LOVE IS DIFFERENT STROKES FOR DIFFERENT FOLKS

GOING FROM IN-LOVE TO LOVING

No one is an expert on the subject of love, especially me. But there is one thing I'm sure of and that is that being 'in love' and 'loving' are two different things.

We do not 'fall in love' with our children, we just love them. And although we might love our friends of the same sex, we do not 'fall in love' with them. (Unless you're that way inclined, that is).

Being 'in love' is like a 100-meter dash. 'Real love' is like a marathon. It is long-haul stuff.

As I see it, after the romantic passion has cooled down to room temperature, we are left with one of two choices — we either 'fall out of love' (whatever that means!) or we choose to start on the process of 'Loving'.

Loving is a *choice*. We can choose to love, or we can choose not to love.

We wake up every morning with that choice.

As mentioned before, love is an act of the mind as much as it is a feeling of the heart.

REAL LOVE HAS NO ROOM FOR PYGMALION CHISELS

When we choose to love — really love — it means 'with no strings attached'. Real Love is warts and all.

Real Love means loving a person for all the qualities in them that we admire, as well as accepting those we don't.

As we saw before, nobody is perfect.

We all have *acceptable* weaknesses. In fact, if we did not have our weaknesses, we would not have our strengths. Our shortcomings are just the shadows of our strengths. But we will talk more about this later.

Real love then, is about letting our partners be just who they are without conditions.

But, for most of us, we do put conditions on our love.

Rather than accepting and loving our loved one for who he or she is, many of us play the 'Pygmalion Game' (both subtle and not so subtle), in an attempt to change them into our idea of who we think they should be.

Please keep in mind that these thoughts come from real life experience. I am a past master, and was a black belt holder, in the art of the Pygmalion Game!

But I'm not alone. In one way, or another, we are all Pygmalion sculptors chiselling away.

If you're married, it's a good idea to forget your faults.

It's no good both of you remembering them.

HOW WE USE OUR PYGMALION CHISELS

The Peacock

The Dove

THE PEACOCK'S MAIN CHISEL

For God's sake! I wish you would lighten up a bit. You take everything so seriously. Don't be so bloody boring. Life is about living and having a bit of fun. In other words, be more like me.

THE DOVE'S MAIN CHISEL

I wish you would be a little more sensitive and caring to other peoples' needs. And I wish you would slow down. Stop and smell the roses more often. In other words, be more like me.

The Eagle

The Owl

THE EAGLE'S MAIN CHISEL

I just don't have the time for this. I really wish you would make some decisions of your own and just get on with it. Get motivated. In other words, be more like me.

THE OWL'S MAIN CHISEL

I wish you would be more careful. You just can't rush into these things like you do without thinking. You have to be on your guard all the time. In other words, be more like me.

Criticism is another way of saying "Why can't you be more like me?"

LET THE PYGMALION GAMES BEGIN!

When we were kids we would try out different little strategies to see how they worked in getting us what we wanted. It wasn't long before we worked out what worked, and what didn't. In the end we had our games down to a fine art. Some of them worked for us nearly every time — you can't win them all — but you can try!

Many of us are still using our child-learnt games way past their use-by-date.

Here are some you might recognise:

Big league Pygmalion Games

- *"I'll go quiet and disappear* — that way I stay right out of trouble."

- *"I'll go quiet, won't talk and get sulky* — it works for me nearly every time."

- *"I'll get loud and throw a tantrum* — it usually works like a treat for me."

- *"I'll get aggressive and bossy* — I win nearly every time."

- *"I'll play the martyr* — *'Oh, well, if you must'* — It gets their attention every time."

- *"Did I tell you what he/she did last night?"* — (rubbishing your partner in front of others).

There are many more games of course. You could probably add a couple more to the list yourself.

WE ALL PLAY THEM

We all play child-like games at one time or another. As I said, we programmed them into the software of our brains when we were kids, and they probably served us very well back then, thank you very much. But the trouble is that by the time we become adults, playing them has become second nature to us. Half the time we don't even know we're doing it. Playing them has become an instinctive and reflex action. We become like robots. Someone pushes the switch — click — we revert to being a child again and — click — we play the game.

Games are a deadly weapon

Games can become deadly weapons in a relationship and when we continue to play them after childhood, they become sharp Pygmalion chisels that we use to chip away at our loved one.

It is impossible to communicate properly, let alone resolve conflict, when one of the partners in a relationship is busy playing a child-like game. It is an even more deadly combination when both partners are playing their favourite game at the same time!

For the 'dance of true communication' to take place in a relationship it requires two adults using all the maturity and intelligence they can muster to make it happen. Unlike the Tango, it only needs one of them to stuff it up. And the quickest way is by playing a game.

The sharpest of chisels

There are many chisels that can be used in the Pygmalion Game. Playing a child-like game is only one of them.

The sharpest of all the chisels is criticism — that most destructive of all personal interchanges. This chisel can take great chunks out with a swift single blow as we use it to sculpt our loved ones into an image of ourselves.

Don't let anyone tell you that there is such a thing as 'constructive criticism' — it does not exist.

Constructive criticism is an oxymoron. No criticism is constructive.

Criticism is a dead-set Pygmalion Game by its definition. Why? Because criticism is literally another way of saying, "Why can't you be more like me?" — you can't get any more Pygmalion than that!

The best way to lose a friend (leave alone a loved one) is to tell them something 'for their own good'.

The 'Criticism Game' is toxic.

The superiority game.

"He lost 80% of his intelligence the day he became a widower."

I like a joke along with the rest of us, but I have to tell you this business of 'one upmanship' (is it now 'one up-personship'? is driving me nuts!

I also believe it is driving a hidden, but real, wedge into a lot of relationships.

When are we going to get over this 'equality' stuff and all gracefully accept that men are men and women are women? When will we accept that it has nothing to do with 'equality' and everything to do with biology? When will we accept that we are just made different? When we do that, then we can admire, respect — and especially — *celebrate* the difference, and get on with the business of living together?

All relationship battles are fought to see who is in charge. In one way or another it is always a power game. It is about balls — who has them and who doesn't.

Note to all women on behalf of all men: Belief by a woman in a man is what makes a man. If it is not his wife, it will be someone else.

(When my wife was reading the manuscript, she wrote alongside the above, 'and vice versa').

The 'Superiority Game' is deadly. And it is one of the quickest ways to hijack a relationship.

Warning: When the games become too much, the partner not playing will look for the exit sign out of the relationship.

If ever there was a book that can change your whole way of looking at relationships it has to be the classic *The Games People Play* by Eric

Berne. Buy it and read it. You will see your relationship (and your friend's relationships) in a whole new and illuminating light. But be warned; if you are a game player (which most of us are) your favourite game will be described in the book, how it is played, and it will show you how you lose when you win. Do yourself and your partner a favour; order it from your nearest bookstore, or on the net. It's a beauty.

8

OUR WINDOWS OF LIFE

Always keep in mind, that no matter how dumb it may look to you, it always makes sense to the person doing it.
It has been said that empathy is the ability to walk in another's shoes. But to have true empathy, you have to take your own off first.

Taking off our shoes starts with being able to see life through the eyes of another person, that is, to see their life-view.

When we can see our partner's life-view it helps us to move into their world. When we can see what they are seeing, it helps us to understand them. And as was mentioned earlier, understanding is everything. It can be the difference between loving or hating.

It strikes me that we spend far too much time in our relationships struggling for agreement. But agreeing with each other is nowhere near as important as understanding where each other is coming from. When we understand each other, then we can agree to disagree without being disagreeable, we can respect each other's point of view.

Of course that doesn't mean to say that we have to necessarily agree with our partner's point of view. We most probably won't. But if we understand each other — when we can see where our partner is coming from — we can get on with the more important stuff in life.

THE VIEW FROM MY WINDOW

Our life views are our windows of life, and each personality style has its own particular view depending on where our window is situated. And each of our views are distorted by our perceptions — the 'waves in the glass' in our particular window.

Whatever we see is real for us. That is why the saying, "Perception is reality" is so true.

We all see life through our own 'lenses of reality' — our windows. And we see a different picture and interpret different meanings from the picture we see. Take the example of the four different personality types witnessing the same car accident. Each will have a different perception of it. Each will notice something different, depending on how they see it.

The Peacock: "Look at that beautiful car — it's been wrecked!"

The Dove: "Gee, I hope nobody's been hurt."

The Eagle: "That little lot's going to cost them about $3,000 each."

The Owl: "If they hadn't been going so fast it would never have happened."

When we treat our partner's view of life as 'wrong' because it is different from our own, it magnifies the problems and causes all sorts of unnecessary stress and conflict. That is why understanding and appreciating that our partner's view of the world is as valid as our own is so important in a relationship.

Perception is reality.

*What I see is true
for me.*

LIFE VIEWS FROM THE DIFFERENT WINDOWS

The Peacock

Life is about living and having fun, live for the moment. Tomorrow's another day and not worth worrying about. Take a few risks and chances. Have a bit of excitement and adventure. You're only here once, but if you do it right, once is all you need.

The Dove

Life is about caring for others. And that includes all the animals, the birds, the trees and everything on this planet. If everybody cared for each other, then we could all live in harmony. Loving and nurturing is the highest ideal of humankind.

The Eagle

Life is about pulling your own weight. There's no free lunch. You either make it happen, or it doesn't happen at all. All the navel-gazing in the world doesn't account for zilch. You have to get off your backside and make things happen. You have to get a result, otherwise, what's the point?

The Owl

Life is a scary business. You have to be on your guard all the time. Be prepared for the worst, because whatever will go wrong will go wrong. That's why you have to have rules and laws to live and work by. You only have to look at all the problems in the world today to see that I'm right.

You can get almost anything you want by giving people what they want.

YOU CAN GET ALMOST ANYTHING YOU WANT

A true relationship begins, and is sustained, when our partner's needs (emotional wants) become as important to us as our own.

But you may well ask: What are my partner's Emotional Wants?

The answer to that question lies in our partner's personality style.

When we understand that, we can then begin to understand and appreciate the Emotional Wants that are part of, and ingrained into, that personality style.

Then if we wish, we can use one of the most powerful (win-win) principles of human nature, which is: 'You can get almost anything you want by giving people (especially your partner) what they want'.

Coupled with this is another principle of dealing with human nature that we looked at earlier, which is; 'People do things for their reasons — not yours — and they always will'.

Sure, people will do things that go against their emotional wants and needs (their reasons). But only for so long. And even then, they will do them only because they *have to*, not because they *want to*.

You don't have to be a psychologist to know that there is a big difference between *having to* and *wanting to*. A *want* comes from within; you do it because you *want* to. A *have to* comes from without, from external pressure. They are the things we are forced to do, rather than what we would choose to do.

Want to's are the things that drive us. They are the things that motivate us. They are the things that *move* us.

The only reason we do *have to's* is to get *want to's*.

For example, most of us *have to* go to work because we *have to* make money, but we do it because the money we make will buy us the things we *want to* have.

- I *have* to go to work because I *want* to live the lifestyle I *want* to live.

- I *have* to have superannuation because I *want* to have security when I'm older.

- I *have* to dress this way because I *want* to look professional/fashionable.

- I *have* to stay in this unhappy relationship because I *want* to appear to be a good wife/husband.

- I *have* to stay in this unhappy relationship because I *want* to be with my kids.

- I *have* to stay in this unhappy relationship because I *want* to be seen as responsible.

- I *have* to stay calm and unassuming because I *want* to have a quiet life.

- I *have* to be loud and forceful because I *want* to be seen as dominant.

- I *have* to be aggressive because I *want* to win.

- I *have* to be always agreeable because I *want* to be seen as caring.

THEIR REASONS

Our partners ultimately do things to satisfy their own emotional wants and needs. It's all part of being human.

When one of the partners is doing more *have to's* than *want to's* in a relationship, you can bet that cracks will start to appear. And like the cracks in a building's foundation, they are more often than not, hidden from view.

A strong loving relationship is formed, and sustained, when both partners' emotional needs are being satisfied more often than they are not.

When you know what your partner's emotional wants are, and you are willing to satisfy them, then you can get almost anything you want.

Sound manipulative? It can be when used in a win-lose manipulative way, but when it's used in a win-win way, it can work magic.

*Logic only makes
me think.*

*It's emotions which
make me act.*

WE ARE NOT LOGICAL CREATURES

I should mention at this point that none of these needs are logical.

Human beings are not logical creatures. We come out of the womb as emotional creatures and we stay that way for the rest of our lives.

Irrespective of what the 'logical' Eagles and Owls of this world will tell you, as I said earlier, nobody has ever made a truly logical decision to do anything. Emotions and feelings are behind every decision we make and every action we take.

The word 'emotion' is derived from the Latin word 'motum', which means, 'to move', 'to set in motion'. It's emotions that move us to take action, not logic. Logic only makes us think, it's emotions that make us act.

So, don't expect logic to feature too much when it comes to why people do the things they do. Oh, sure, we make our decisions sound logical. But we can rationalise anything (make it sound logical) if we really want to. Remember, we make the facts fit our fictions. We make the head give reasons for what the heart really wants to do. We do things because they feel right — not because they are right.

Happiness is when our emotional wants are being fulfilled.

Unhappiness is when they are not.

THE EMOTIONAL WANTS OF THE FOUR STYLES

THE TALKER

Wants to be the centre of attention
Wants to be noticed
Wants to be popular
Wants recognition and praise
Wants constant compliments
Wants to be famous

THE FEELER

Wants approval and acceptance
Wants to be caring
Wants to belong
Wants to be supportive
Wants to be needed
Wants to be loved

THE DOER

Wants to be in control
Wants to take command
Wants to call the shots
Wants to be independent
Wants to win

THE THINKER

Wants stability
Wants life to be predictable
Wants structure
Wants things to stay the same
Wants security

We do things because they feel right, not because they are right.

If it wasn't for marriage husbands and wives would have to quarrel with strangers.

9

CONFLICTS AND QUARRELS

A woman told me the other day that she and her husband have an agreement. They never go to sleep angry with each other.
She said she has now been awake for nearly six months!

What is conflict?

Conflict happens when we feel somebody is trying to take something away from us; our time, our money, our power, our dignity, our reputation etc. In other words, it is a feeling that someone is 'trespassing against us' and we feel threatened. And like all other creatures, we will either fight or flight or freeze.

Each of us has our preferred strategy, or defence mechanism, when we feel threatened. Some of us fight, some of us flight, and some of us freeze.

Like everything else, the different personality styles have fairly predictable habits of acting and reacting to threats.

Generally speaking, the different personality styles' self-defence mechanisms look something like the following.

SELF-DEFENCE MECHANISMS

When threatened, we fight, flight or freeze

The Peacock

Fights first by becoming loud, emotional and dramatic. Then flights by quickly wanting to become friends again.

I was only joking. Are we still friends?

The Dove

Flights first by being agreeable and compliant to avoid conflict. Then fights by becoming quietly stubborn and digging in.

Let's try and keep the peace. Anything for a quiet life.

The Eagle

Fights first with blunt coolness and logic, often with added biting sarcasm. Then flights by avoiding the issue or the person causing the aggravation.

Let's get on with the more important things.

The Owl

Flights first by becoming even more cool and withdrawn. Then fights by becoming, self-righteous with a holier-than-thou attitude.

Everything would be alright if you just did it my way.

CLASHING PERSONALITIES

More often than not, the people we find hard to get along with are normally our 'diagonal opposites' because we tend to see their weaknesses, rather than their strengths.

Interestingly enough, research and experience show that not only is the old saying, 'opposites attract' true, but it also shows that they generally have very enduring relationships. Perhaps it's because each partner brings to the relationship things that the other partner doesn't have, which can provide a nice balance.

Look at that boring fussy person. Wouldn't get excited if there was a fire in the building. What a pain! Why can't they be more like me?

Look at that overpowering bossy Hitler. Always angry. Fancy living with that! Why can't they be more like me?

What a wimp! Weak and wishy-washy. Lets people walk all over them. A real doormat. No initiative that's the problem. Why can't they be more like me?

What a loud-mouthed show-off! Empty, frivolous, flamboyant and a general pain in the ...! Why can't they be more like me?

"I'm Sorry"

**An apology is better than
an explanation and
a lot quicker.**

NOBODY CAN REALLY UPSET US UNLESS WE LET THEM

Let's be honest, after a time we all become experts at being able to manipulate our partner's emotions. We know just what buttons to push — either positively or negatively.

At times when we are playing our Pygmalion games it is hard to work out who is doing what to whom. So it doesn't hurt us to be on our guard with a bit of armour.

One of the best pieces of armour we can use to protect ourselves is also one of the most powerful principles I have ever learnt, and that is:

Nobody can upset us unless we let them.

The choice is always ours

We can choose how we react.

The difference between a child and a mature adult (and it has nothing to do with age) is in their ability to control their emotions. When a child is upset it immediately triggers an emotional reaction. They go from feeling straight to action. In other words, they react without thinking. But they're allowed to — they're kids.

Making a choice (thinking first) of how we will act and react when somebody upsets us is what makes us an adult. We have a choice. We can stop, *think*, then *choose* how we will react.

Without emotional control, without choosing how we react, we become like a child and put ourselves straight in the hands of anyone (fool or otherwise) who can make us lose our cool.

But he/she upsets me!

"He upsets me!"

"She upsets me!"

Nobody can upset us unless we choose to let them. Choice is the ultimate armour. We have the ability to make choices about our own emotions. We are always responsible for how we feel.

We are what we think. We feel what we think. And we can learn to think differently about anything if we decide to. Easy to do? No! If it was, everybody would be doing it. But it really is worth the effort of trying.

Some of those old Greeks said some pretty wise things. One I especially like is by Aristotle, who said:

"Anyone can become angry — that is easy. But to be angry with the right person, to the right degree, at the right time, for the right purpose, and in the right way — that is not easy."

When an argument looms, the best weapon to hold is your tongue. There is none so wise as the person who says nothing at the right time. In other words, sometimes the best way to save face when it comes to a potential argument is to keep the bottom half of it closed!

The strongest of armour

The strongest armour we can have is a high level of self-esteem, that is; self-confidence, which is governed by how much we like ourselves. When our self-esteem is high the arrows of criticism harmlessly bounce off us. The opposite is also true. When our self-esteem is low, we become vulnerable and easily wounded by any fool, or otherwise, who wants to load their bow and shoot.

For the masochists

Having said that 'nobody can upset us unless we let them', if you are a masochist, on the next page are some sure-fire ways of getting up the noses of the different styles.

Or for those who want to avoid giving their partner pain, here are some good things to avoid doing.

HATES OF THE FOUR STYLES

The Peacock

HATES
Not being centre stage
Not being noticed
Being criticised
Being disciplined
Permanence
Sameness
Being bored

The Dove

HATES
Rejection
Being alone
Not being needed
Conflict
Aggressiveness
Not being loved
Being hurried

The Eagle

HATES
Being dependent
Being told what to do
Long explanations
Being seen as weak
Being wrong
Emotional displays
Excuses
Losing

The Owl

HATES
Uncertainty
Insecurity
Lack of rules
Change
Not being right
Taking risks
Emotional displays
Making quick decisions

*A weakness is simply
a strength that has
been taken
too far.*

10

DO YOU KNOW WHAT REALLY ANNOYS ME?

I asked a young woman, "What did you do before you were married?"
To which she replied, "Anything I wanted to do!"

One of the biggest strategies used in the Pygmalion Game is 'helping' our partner to overcome his or her shortcomings, their 'character weaknesses'. This is done 'for their own good', of course. It helps to make them 'better people'. And they're just so much easier to live with.

Thereby is the crux of it – *they are just so much easier to live with*.

This brings us right back to an earlier point; *we do things for our own reasons*, not for someone else's. Remember, if you are going to bet on the human race, always back self-interest to win — because it will every time!

Helping our loved one to overcome their 'weaknesses' is an important chisel in the Pygmalion tool kit. No self-respecting Pygmalion could do without it. And as I have said before, we are all Pygmalion sculptors in one way or another.

Picking up on a point made earlier, a weakness totally depends on who is looking, and in what situation it is being used at the time. For instance:

- **The Peacock** talks too much. But that could be good if you are trying to talk your way out of a tight spot. Watch almost any Eddie Murphy film.

- **The Eagle** is too sharp and bossy. But that could be good in a tight situation. Watch any 'Dirty Harry' movie.

- **The Dove** is too sensitive and non-assertive. But that could be good if you are needing sensitivity and support. Watch almost any Robin Williams movie.

- **The Owl** is too conservative and rule-bound. But that is good when you are trying to bring some sort of structure and stability to a situation.

Often, as we take up our Pygmalion chisels, we don't realise that as we chip away at the 'weaknesses', we are also chiselling into the body of the statue.

As I have said before, strength and weakness go together. It is because of our strengths that we have our weaknesses. In a nutshell, a weakness is simply a strength that we have taken too far. It is only when we take our strengths too far, and they get out of balance, that they are seen as a weakness.

STRENGTHS AND SHORTCOMINGS

The Peacock

STRENGTHS
Optimistic
Energetic
Fun-loving
Imaginative

SHORTCOMINGS
Excitable
Undisciplined
Talks too much

The Dove

STRENGTHS
Calm
Caring
Loyal
Patient

SHORTCOMINGS
Oversensitive
Easily manipulated
Slow to act

The Eagle

STRENGTHS
Confident
Decisive
Independent
Disciplined

SHORTCOMINGS
Impatient
Bossy
Critical

The Owl

STRENGTHS
Careful
Steady
Reliable
Systematic

SHORTCOMINGS
Over-cautious
Rule-bound
Self-righteous

*Please God, give me
patience, and
I want it
NOW!*

The Peacock

COMMON PARTNER COMPLAINTS ABOUT THE PEACOCK

- Gets too emotional and excitable.
- Too outgoing and loud — draws attention.
- Needs to be amused and entertained all the time.
- Wants to always be the centre of attention — shows off.
- Wants to entertain all the time — we always have people around.
- Doesn't pay enough attention to details — careless.
- Won't stick to something — good starter but a poor finisher.
- Exaggerates — to the point of telling lies.
- Flies off the handle too quickly — a loud quick temper.
- Messy and untidy — won't clean up.
- Boastful — uses too many sentences starting with "I."
- Terrible with money — always in debt.
- Unpredictable — never know what's next.
- Flirts — but says it doesn't mean anything.
- Takes too many risks — especially with way out business ideas.
- Drives too fast — reckless.
- Self-centred — preoccupied with looks and dress.
- Disorganised — in thinking and personal habits.
- Impatient — won't wait for anything.
- Too many pipe dreams – not realistic.

The Dove

COMMON PARTNER COMPLAINTS ABOUT THE DOVE

- Doesn't take a logical approach to problems.
- Personalises things — too sensitive and emotional.
- Wants too much of my time — crowds me.
- Gets used up by others — too accommodating, can't say no.
- Unmotivated — too much of a follower.
- Too dependant — won't initiate anything alone.
- Over-apologetic — apologises for everything, including all the world wars!
- Too self-critical — unsure, lacks self-esteem and confidence.
- Procrastinates — keeps putting things off.
- Idealistic — sees the world through rose coloured glasses.
- Too trusting — lets others take advantage.
- Too deep — won't share deepest thoughts and feelings.
- Chatterer — rabbits on about nothing.
- Habit-bound — won't take risks.
- Too shy — won't push forward.
- Won't argue — won't clear the air.
- Withdraws — goes into shell when hurt.

The Eagle

COMMON PARTNER COMPLAINTS ABOUT THE EAGLE

- Too insensitive — unemotional, unfeeling.
- Blunt — too quick and to the point.
- Arrogant — rude.
- Too independent — doesn't need me.
- Always preoccupied thinking — doesn't listen.
- Always gives a quick answer instead of discussing the problem.
- Can become very bossy, sharp and sarcastic when up tight.
- Wants to rule the roost — wants to make all the decisions.
- Impatient — won't wait for anything.
- Workaholic — totally driven by any current project.
- Critical — no patience for normal human frailties.
- Doesn't like to be questioned — their word is law.

The Owl

COMMON PARTNER COMPLAINTS ABOUT THE OWL

- Emotionally distant — seems uncaring.
- Takes life far too seriously — never lightens up.
- Too up-tight and inhibited — can't let go and play.
- Too introverted — to the point of being anti-social.
- Has little sense of humour — doesn't laugh enough.
- Conversation is always too heavy — doesn't like to just chat.
- Won't discuss feelings and emotional issues — stays distant.
- Isn't romantic — lacks passion and imagination.
- Too tied to a set routine — won't vary from it.
- Has to write lists for everything — drives me crazy.
- Too cautious about everything — won't take a chance.
- Too conservative and straight-laced — boring.
- Fault-finding and critical — acts more like a parent than a partner.
- Explains everything in fine boring detail — drives me nuts.
- Too mean with money; won't splurge now and again.
- Has to keep checking everything — drives me to distraction.
- Too suspicious of other peoples' good intentions.
- Impatient and intolerant of normal human weaknesses.
- Can hold a long simmering grudge.

11

RELATIONSHIP STRATEGIES

"You know, when I'm with you it's just like having on old joggers."

"Thank you very much — I don't think!"

"It's not meant to be an insult. It's meant to be a compliment. What I'm trying to say is that when I'm with you, I can just be me — it's comfortable."

As a friend of mine confided in me recently, "Oh, for a partner that lets me just be myself, who expects nothing of me other than that I should just be me. What a partner that would be!"

When we feel totally comfortable in another's company; when we feel no need to watch what we say; when we feel no need to be guarded in how we act; when we feel no need to put on our 'outside world face'. When all that happens, we know we have a *true* relationship with that person.

One more time: A true relationship begins, and is sustained, when both partners realise that the other partner's needs are as important as their own, and attempts to fulfil those needs.

But I am the first to admit that it's not always easy to do.

Part of the problem is the fact that we are naturally self-preoccupied creatures.

We think about ourselves around 98 per cent of the time.

Even when we are thinking of others, it is normally in relation to ourselves.

*When I'm with you,
I feel comfortable
enough to
be me.*

There is nothing wrong with that, it is just part of being human. The problem though, is that we can become so preoccupied with our own needs that we sometimes forget our loved one's needs are just as important — perhaps even more important as far as the relationship is concerned.

The following are some Relationship Strategies for living harmoniously with the different personality styles.

The Peacock

RELATIONSHIP STRATEGIES FOR LIVING WITH THE PEACOCK

Peacocks are confident, outgoing, friendly, talkative, enthusiastic, optimistic, witty and happy-go-lucky people who will be in anything that looks like fun, particularly where other people are involved and especially where they can be the centre of attention. They like to have excitement and variety in their lives. They are driven by the need for recognition and praise.

Some 'Do' strategies:

Oh, for a partner that lets me just be myself, who expects nothing of me other than that I should just be me. What a partner that would be!

♦ Do accept that they are the most dramatic and emotionally expressive of all people. That's why Peacocks make such great actors.

♦ Do be optimistic and up-beat when you are with them. Negativity and pessimism is poison to them — and they hate to be around it.

♦ Do accept that they like to touch and cuddle — a lot.

♦ Do accept the fact that they like talking about themselves — it's their favourite subject!

♦ Do accept the fact that they exaggerate things and can tend to handle the truth a little carelessly. They don't let the facts get in the way of what they're trying to get across.

♦ Do let them showoff and be the centre of attention — it's their favourite pastime! Remember, inside of all Peacocks is an entertainer busting to get out.

- Do give them lots of encouragement, praise and compliments — it's their oxygen, it keeps them alive.

- Do understand that they are unpredictable, disorganised, and can be unreliable, especially about doing something they said they would do before they had a sleep on it.

- Do accept that they crack jokes when you think they should be serious. They do this to ease the tension when they're under pressure.

- Do appreciate that they are terrible at handling money. They are 'live for today and let tomorrow take care of itself' people.

- Do accept that when they're down, they're really down. They have very high highs and very low lows.

- Do help them to think a situation through by using a little more logic and analytical judgement.

- Do tell them you love them about every ten minutes — they like constant reassurance!

Some 'Don't' strategies:

These are also some of the 'rough edges' that Pygmalion chiselers like to chip away at.

- Don't expect them to take a logical approach to things. They won't. They are governed by their heart — their feelings — not by their head.

- Don't expect them to be good with details. They're not. They hate them.

- Don't expect them to settle into a boring routine or be a homebody. They won't. They want their life to be full of variety.

- Don't expect them to be good listeners. They're not. They gain energy talking and lose energy listening. It actually tires them out.

- Don't be over-critical about them being impractical with money. They already know they are.

- Don't pour cold water on their dreams and ambitions. It's what keeps them going.

- Don't expect them to take things lying down. They won't. They are the most emotionally reactive of all the styles.

- Don't expect them to keep doing good things without constant praise. Almost everything they do is for the reward of praise.

- Don't expect them to let you have the last word. It won't happen!

The Dove

RELATIONSHIP STRATEGIES FOR LIVING WITH THE DOVE

Doves are shy, friendly, sensitive, compassionate, caring, reliable and supportive people. They care about the welfare of others. Everything is done low-key and in moderation. They have a close circle of comfortable and non-threatening friends and like to stick close to home. They want to live a life of caring which is full of love and friendships. They are driven by the need for acceptance and approval.

Some 'Do' strategies:

Oh, for a partner that lets me just be myself, who expects nothing of me other than that I should just be me. What a partner that would be!

♦ Do appreciate that they want their life to be lived in harmony and peace. They like calm. To the Dove, these are the riches of life — not money or a flash car.

♦ Do understand that they flourish in a happy, stable and predictable environment with no threat of sudden changes or disruptions.

♦ Do appreciate that they are the most caring and compassionate of all the styles and expect others to be the same.

♦ Do understand that they are 'feelers,' not 'thinkers' and therefore make their decisions based on intuition and feeling rather than logic.

♦ Do understand that they will do almost anything to avoid conflict and aggression. In a disagreement, if they retreat and go quiet, you haven't won — you've lost — especially if you shout.

♦ Do understand that their goal in life is to belong, to be needed, and to be loved. Reassure them how much you need them.

- Do appreciate that they are the most sensitive of all the styles. They can be hurt and embarrassed by things that some of the other styles wouldn't give a second thought to.

- Do understand that they can be acutely embarrassed by being the centre of attention in public. Avoid pushing them into the spotlight.

- Do appreciate that they may be hesitant to verbally express their affection, but will express it in other ways, especially in being supportive and doing 'kind deeds' for those they care about.

- Do understand that they will not speak up for themselves. Sometimes you have to be their guardian.

- Do appreciate that because they are deep and sensitive, but also introverted and quiet, sometimes their problems can get the best of them. Be a shoulder to lean on.

- Do understand that if you are an Eagle then the Dove will disagree with whatever you say out of sheer principle!

Some 'Don't' strategies:

These are also some of the 'rough edges' that Pygmalion chiselers like to chip away at.

- Don't expect them to take a logical approach to things. They can't. And they won't. They are driven by their feelings.

- Don't expect them to be assertive and stand up for themselves. It won't happen. It's against everything they stand for.

- Don't expect them to be the boss, or to tell other people what to do in a disciplinary way. That too won't happen for the same reason mentioned above.

- Don't expect them to make decisions or take risks. They won't. They spend their lives double-guessing themselves as it is, without you giving them any added worries!

- Don't rush them into anything. Give them plenty of time to weigh up the pro's and con's of anything that looks like change or risk.

- Don't expect them to be comfortable in the public eye. It's the last place in the world they want to be.

- Don't expect them to initiate or take the lead. They are far more comfortable 'going along with it' than 'making it happen.'

- Don't criticise them for being too casual. You may see their casualness as a liability. Many see it as an asset.

- Don't criticise others, especially their friends. They are the ultimate 'live and let live' people.

- Don't ever question their loyalty. To the Dove, loyalty is always spelt in capital letters — and underlined.

The Eagle

RELATIONSHIP STRATEGIES FOR LIVING WITH THE EAGLE

Eagles are independent, confident, fast, assertive no-nonsense people who are always in a hurry. Extremely goal-centred and competitive, they normally display a detached sense of urgency. They are usually mentally 'somewhere else,' always preoccupied with a work problem or some current project. Their lives are spent striving for achievement. They are driven by getting results — fast.

Some 'Do' strategies:

Oh, for a partner that lets me just be myself, who expects nothing of me other than that I should just be me. What a partner that would be!

- ♦ Do understand that being in control of things is how they get their sense of security; they need to be in charge. So, if it does no more than harm your ego, then let them be (or appear to be) in control. The word 'boss' was invented for them!

- ♦ Do understand that they are highly competitive and are 'win at all costs' people. They will debate issues with you aggressively just for the sheer fun of the game. Don't worry about it, they are aggressively enthusiastic with everything they do. It is rarely personal.

- ♦ Do appreciate that they are independent self-starters who will take risks. Be prepared for a fast and changing ride. Homebodies they ain't.

- ♦ Do understand that they are optimistic positive thinkers and are turned off by pessimistic and negative people. Moaning and complaining people are to be avoided at all costs.

- ♦ Do understand that they are sharp-minded quick thinkers and decision makers. They will think-decide-act while everybody else is still thinking about it. Sometimes their decisions are not always the best for everyone concerned, but at least they're quick!

- Do accept that they are workaholics, that their career invariably comes first. To the Eagle, work is play and play is work.

- Do understand that feelings, and especially being guided by them, is a totally foreign concept to them — they do not understand how to deal with them. Forget trying to use emotional appeals to persuade them into anything.

- Do understand that they are emotionally controlled and show few outward emotions or feelings. But deep down they are extremely protective about those they care for.

Some 'Don't' strategies:

These are also some of the 'rough edges' that Pygmalion chiselers like to chip away at.

- Don't expect them to be good listeners. They're not, and they never will be.

- Don't expect them to be mushy and cry in sad movies. It won't happen.

- Don't be possessive or clingy. They admire independence and strength of will.

- Don't try and be bossy or lay down the rules. Eagles hate rules. Eagles make the rules for everybody else — not for themselves!

- Don't expect them to suffer long-winded explanations, idle chatter, and especially excuses. They detest all three in about equal proportions.

- Don't expect them to take holidays where they can 'just do nothing and relax.' That's more like hell than heaven for the Eagle.

- Don't expect them to explain their decisions and actions. They know they should, but they hate having to do it.

- Don't expect them to be patient and tolerant. They can't even spell the words!

- Don't be timid with them, and don't beat about the bush with them. They're decisive, positive up-front people and they wish everybody else was the same.

- Don't be upset by their sarcasm or knife-edged comments when they get up-tight. It's all part of their make-up. Take solace in the fact that once it's said, it's over. They rarely think too long about it or harbour a grudge.

- Don't ever break a promise or commitment to them. To the Eagle, your word is your bond.

The Owl

RELATIONSHIP STRATEGIES FOR LIVING WITH THE OWL

Owls are conservative, reserved, and quiet people. They can often appear detached and aloof. They generally like to do things alone and uninterrupted. Cautious and somewhat pessimistic, they can be obsessively meticulous, especially in their desire for detail. They prefer to live a safe, orderly and structured life based on set routines with no sudden surprises. They are driven by the need for certainty. They need to be right.

Some 'Do' strategies:

Oh, for a partner that lets me just be myself, who expects nothing of me other than that I should just be me. What a partner that would be!

- Do appreciate that Owls live by 'old fashioned values' which they hold dear. They have strong opinions of right and wrong. There are few, if any, shades of grey in the Owl's world when it comes to how people should conduct themselves.

- Do understand that they are not social creatures. They prefer to stay close to the privacy (and solitude) of their own home. Forget any wild parties.

- Do appreciate that they take life very seriously. Many seem to have had a 'humour bypass' operation. They especially take themselves very seriously and have little, if any, ability to be able to laugh at themselves. Forget the jokes.

- Do understand they are not emotionally outward people, they keep their feelings buried deep and to themselves, and they expect others to do the same thing.

- Do understand that they are first and foremost logical creatures, their strength lies in being analytical, not in being intuitive or imaginative. Why anyone would want to do something based on emotions or feelings is completely beyond them. They do not understand it, or how to deal with it. Forget trying to use emotional appeals to persuade them into anything.

- Do appreciate that they are basically independent loners. They like their own company and they need their solitude. They need distance from other people so that they can 'do their own thing' quietly and without distractions. Give them space.

- Do understand that they can be disciplinarians who set rules which they believe should be followed, both by themselves and those close to them. Be prepared to obey the rules.

- Do appreciate that they live their life strictly by set routines and patterns — habits. And that they feel insecure and extremely uncomfortable when they are prevented from following them.

- Do understand that Owls are thinkers who want to be right in everything they do, do not like change or disruption to their normal way of doing things, and see change as a risk that should be avoided. If you suggest any sort of change, always make sure you give them plenty of time to think, along with plenty of information about it (preferably on paper), and be prepared for a long wait!

- Do appreciate that as with everything they do, Owls take their relationships very seriously. They are strong, steady, 'Rock of Gibraltar' partners who possess a fierce loyalty and devotion to those they care about.

Some 'Don't' strategies:

These are also some of the 'rough edges' that Pygmalion chiselers like to chip away at.

- Don't expect them to change their habits and set routines. They won't.

- Don't expect them to take any risks. It's against everything they believe in.

- Don't expect them to stop writing lists of things they have to do. They won't stop. To the Owl, it doesn't exist unless it's on paper. They love paper.

- Don't try and push them into making a quick decision. You'll get an immediate (and 'safe') 'no' that might have been a 'yes' if you had given them more time to think.

- Don't expect spontaneous acts of emotion, passion or romantic gestures. They will not happen.

- Don't expect them to ever admit that they might not know something. The Owl knows everything and has an opinion on everything.

- Don't expect them to think that they might be wrong about something. The Owl is never wrong. Never.

- Don't expect them to be tolerant about normal human frailties. It won't happen. In fact they can be quite puritan and 'holier than thou' when it comes to human weaknesses.

- Don't expect them to know what you want by using terms such as, "Well, you know what I mean...? They don't. Be specific. Spell it out.

- Don't expect that you can win an argument with an Owl by being emotional. You won't. They have no idea why you should be emotional, they do not understand it, they can't handle it, and they don't see it as a valid. You lose.

*Communication has nothing
to do with what is said,
only with what
is received.*

12

COMMUNICATING

"I did not say that."
"No, but that's what you meant!"
"I know you believe you understand what you think I said, but I'm not sure you realise that what you heard is not what I meant!"

Sound familiar?

There is little doubt that most psychologists and marriage guidance counsellors agree that the major underlying reason why most relationships fracture at the seams is through communication — or lack of it — or the wrong sort of communication.

It has always struck me as almost unbelievable that schools teach children just about everything except one of the most important things they will need; how to communicate effectively. Yet we spend a good deal of our lives doing just that — communicating. In fact how well we communicate dictates to a large degree just how successful we will be in life generally; let alone in a relationship.

One of the problems with communication is that it only means what it means to the other person. It has nothing to do with what is said, or not said. It only has to do with what the other person receives. In other words, the only meaning of our communication is the response we get from it.

Communication is such a tricky business. Sometimes we are damned if we do, and damned if we don't.

The quiet types

First we have the deep and quiet types like the Doves and the Owls. They are great listeners, but not so good at expressing themselves. They hardly say anything. They seem to assume that people are either mind readers, or that you wouldn't understand even if they told you. The problem is that we are not mind readers.

If two people cannot express their deep feelings with each other there will always be a barrier in the relationship. Silence creates emotional distance. Hiding separates. Openness unites.

The talker types

Then we have the talker types, like the Peacocks and the Eagles. They are good talkers, but terrible listeners. They not only do not listen, but shoot straight from the lip. They say just what they're thinking without thinking.

And as the old saying goes; 'Words are like arrows. Once flung into the air they cannot be returned'.

ARE YOU LISTENING TO ME?

"Why don't you ever listen!?"

The answer to that one is that for most of us, but especially for the Peacocks and the Eagles, listening is hard. It is a totally unnatural act for them. A Peacock friend of mine reckons that "Listening is a totally unnatural act!"

The problem of 'really listening' for the Peacocks comes about because they are so preoccupied with their own thoughts and feelings. They want to tell you how they feel, not listen to how you feel. Listening without talking (especially about themselves) for any length of time is like digging holes to the Peacock – it absolutely exhausts them.

Peacocks do better when they heed the old ditty:

> Mouth I've one and ears I've two,
>   Well that's what I got the last count,
> Perhaps somebody is trying to tell us
>   We should use them in the same amount.

Eagles do not listen well because they think they are so logical and objective. So, when the conversation turns to emotional issues — and you can't get anything more illogical and subjective than an emotional issue! — they become impatient and irritated with the non-objectivity of it all. Listening for any length of time about emotional issues irritates the Hell out of them. They just don't see the point of it all.

Eagles do better when they keep in mind that people are not rational and logical (including them). In fact, as I have said before, we are born emotional creatures and stay that way for the rest of our lives.

Even if Eagles can't come to grips with this fact of life, it would pay them to know that one of the greatest compliments you can give to another human being is to truly listen to them.

WHY DON'T YOU TALK TO ME?

"Why don't you talk to me – why don't you tell me what's on your mind?"

For most of us, expressing our thoughts about our emotions is hard. But it is especially hard for the Doves and the Owls. To them, talking about, and being able to express their innermost feelings and thoughts is like having a tooth pulled — without anesthetic!

The problem of expressing their innermost feelings for the Dove is that they are hypersensitive; both to talking about how they feel ("It's embarrassing") and to the possibility that it could cause a conflict situation — which they will avoid, no matter what the cost.

The problem of expressing their innermost feelings for the Owl is that they are the 'deep, silent types,' they like to keep their feelings to themselves. The Owl can also tend to see expressing any sign of outward emotion as 'weak' or 'improper.' Keeping a stiff upper lip is important to the Owl.

When it's all said and done, problems in a relationship don't just go away. They have to be talked through, and listened through, and worked through, or else they will always remain a barrier to the relationship. The old saying rings true, especially in a relationship: "If you are not part of the solution, then you are part of the problem".

If you want to read two beautiful books about some of the things we have just been talking about, buy and read *Why Am I Afraid To Love?* and *Why I Am Afraid To Tell You Who I Am* both written by John Powell. They are two little books that can change your life and your relationships. Order them in from your nearest bookstore, or get them on the net.

In the meantime, let's look at how the different personalities 'naturally' communicate.

COMMUNICATION STYLES

We communicate with others the way we would like to be communicated to.

The Peacock

Talks fast
Strong voice
Expressive face
Dramatic gestures
Witty
Poor listener
Will interrupt speaker

They want to talk about themselves, doesn't listen

The Dove

Softly spoken
Self-conscious
Bashful
Modest
Expressive face
Easy to talk to
Good listener

Intimately bashful when talking about emotional issues

The Eagle

Talks fast
To the point
No nonsense
No small talk
Can seem blunt
Poor listener
Will interrupt speaker

Quick, abrupt and to the point, wants to deal with facts, not emotions

The Owl

Softly spoken
Quiet
Non-expressive face
Can seem detached
Slow to respond
Good listener
Can seem like a closed book

Intimately reserved when it comes to talking about emotional issues

Feeling gratitude and not expressing it is like wrapping a gift and not giving it.

WE SPEAK A DIFFERENT LANGUAGE

We communicate for different reasons. We use a different 'currency'. We come from a 'different world'. And we speak in a different language.

No wonder we have so much trouble communicating with each other.

If we can see and understand where our partner is coming from it can help us to overcome a lot of the hassles that communication between the different styles can often cause.

Eagles and Owls come from an internal world of logic. Their currency is facts. They deal in facts, not feelings. Their language is impersonal, precise, objective and factual.

Peacocks and Doves come from an internal world of emotions. Their currency is feelings. They deal in feelings, not facts. Their language is personal, emotional and expressive.

Because Eagles and Owls deal in facts, not feelings, when having a conversation they will search for the facts in what is being said — 'what is the truth of the matter?' — and will attempt to stay as objective (and impersonal) as possible, in order to filter out any emotions and feelings (both their own and others) which could cloud the issue. They will ask questions in order to understand and clarify the logic behind what is being said. Eagles and Owls look for the facts when they are communicating.

Because Peacocks and Doves deal in feelings, not facts, when having a conversation they will search for the feelings behind what is being said — 'what is being felt here?' — and will attempt to become personally involved in what the other person is saying. They will ask questions in order to find common ground and share experiences. Peacocks and Doves look for the feelings when they are communicating.

Nowhere do these two different ways of communicating show up more dramatically than in a disagreement between the styles. The Peacock and the Dove will see the disagreement as personal — being between them and their partner. The Eagle and the Owl will see the argument as impersonal — simply being between two different positions, or points of view.

Let's have a look at some examples.

Owl: "I think it's time we gave some thought to selling the holiday shack and investing the money in something that will give us a better return on our investment."

Peacock: "Why would you want to sell the holiday shack?"

Owl: "I just told you why. We can get a lot better return placing the money in some shares, plus the money we'll save by not having to maintain it."

Peacock: "But I love that shack! We've had some really good times there, the kids grew up going there every year. It's full of great memories. There's nowhere on earth that I feel as happy and relaxed as I do at the shack. We can't sell it!"

Owl: "You're getting too emotional about it. It's only a shack for goodness sake, and it's not getting any younger. The cost of maintaining it is getting more every year — and besides I think the kids are getting a bit sick of going there, anyway."

Peacock: "Rubbish! The kids love it — and so do I. Don't you have any sentimental feelings for it?"

Owl: "Of course I do, but you have to be rational about things like this. We have to think about our future as well. The money we get for it could build up into a nice little nest egg down the track if we invest it wisely."

Peacock: "There's more to life than money you know. I really look forward to going to that shack — I love that shack — we can't sell it!"

Owl: "I think you're being overly emotional about the whole thing."

Peacock: "You would."... etc. etc. etc.

The different ways we communicate also shows up when it comes to helping someone solve a problem. The Peacock and the Dove will generally get the other person to 'talk it through' and help them come up with their own answer to the problem, acting like a counsellor. The Eagle and the Owl on the other hand will generally deliver (and fairly quickly) an answer to the other person's problem, acting more like a teacher.

Dove: "I'm getting sick of doing the maintenance on our shack. It's costing us more each year and I'm tired of travelling up there to do it."

Eagle: "Let's sell it, then."

Dove: "Sell it! But I love that shack!"

Eagle: "Well why are you complaining about it, then?"

Dove: "I'm just telling you I'm sick of working on it — not that I want to sell it. We have a lot of happy memories invested in that shack. I wouldn't even consider selling it."

Eagle: "Well stop moaning about it."

Dove: "Your impossible to have a sensible conversation with!"

If we keep in mind that we are coming from different worlds and dealing in different currencies — the currency of facts for the Eagle and Owl, and the currency of feelings for the Peacock and Dove — and that each of our currencies have just as much value as the other, it can help us avoid an awful lot of misunderstandings and heartaches when it comes to our relationships.

*Money can't buy
you happiness.*

*That's why we have
credit cards.*

13

THE MONEY WARS

"It's time we bought a new car, I reckon we should go for one of those four-wheel drive jobs, what do you think?"

"I think we should wait for a while, until we can better afford it, and anyway, why a new one, and why a four-wheel drive?"

Who is doing the talking? Which one wants to buy the new car, the man or the woman?

"I can't stand this brand of cheese, it tastes soapy to me. Why don't you buy the better brand?"

"The better brand costs $1.30 more, and anyway, I don't reckon there's any difference between them."

Who is doing the talking? Which one wants to buy the 'better' brand of cheese, the man or the woman?

The answers to these quiz questions can be found on page 165 — only joking.

In the first case, it is the woman who wants to buy the new car. In the second case, it is the man who bought the cheese.

If you're over 45, those answers may surprise you. If you're not, they won't.

Because many (most?) couples are now opting for a different approach to their relationships than their parents had, and because many are also going for a completely different lifestyle to the one their parents lived, things have changed dramatically on the home front.

Women are working, often long hours, and in some cases bringing home more money than their male partners.

On the other hand, men are more involved with the domestic side of things; preparing meals, picking up the kids from school or the crèche, doing the housework, buying the food and a dozen other things. The line between 'what a man and a woman does' has not only blurred, but in some cases, disappeared altogether.

Suddenly both partners rightly want a say in where the dollars go. The man is having more of a say in the brands of food being bought, the choice of clothes for the kids, what presents to buy. The woman is having more of a say in where the money should be spent, what car they should buy, and when. It can be fertile ground for resentment, arguments, and especially game playing to breed. And it appears that is exactly what seems to be happening.

According to a survey conducted by Relationships Australia, there has been a dramatic increase in the type of arguments that couples are having. And they're generally about power and money.

And according to the results of the 'Great Australian Sex and Relationship Survey' conducted in late 1990s, this is what the top eight arguments are about:

1. Money: 43%
2. Lack of time together: 35%
3. Kids: 30%
4. Other: 26%
5. Sex: 24%
6. Work: 21%
7. In-laws: 15%
8. Other people: 15%

From a personality point of view, we can predict with a fair amount of certainty who will be doing what — and why — in these 'Money Wars'.

The Peacock

THE PEACOCK AND MONEY

"You never let poverty get in the way of a good time."

Remember, the Peacock is driven by the need for recognition and applause. And that is just what money can buy them.

The Peacock will want to spend money on things that their partner (if not another Peacock) may well see as extravagant, even luxurious, and certainly far too expensive.

Peacocks want to have 'nice things' around them (clothes, toys and creature comforts) and they want them *now*, irrespective of whether, or not, they can afford them.

The Peacock wants instant gratification. "Bung it on the credit card, we'll worry about paying for it later. Loosen up a bit. Live for today, tomorrow we could all be dead!"

The big problem is that if you don't die, you have to pay the bills!

If the Peacock is married to another Peacock then their credit cards (you can bet they will have several) will generally all be at their limit.

If the Peacock is married to a Dove, then the Dove's stomach is constantly in a knot through worrying about paying the bills.

If the Peacock is married to the controlling Eagle, they normally quite happily work out how they will handle their money. The Eagle will see to that.

If the Peacock is married to the careful and cautious Owl, then the scene is set for lots of 'money wars' and the Owl suffering more headaches and constipation than normal.

The Dove

THE DOVE AND MONEY

"Money makes me feel safer."

Remember, the Dove is driven by the need for approval and belonging. And that is just what money can buy them.

The Dove is careful with their money, but not quite as careful as the Owl — no one is!

The most supportive and accommodating of all the styles, the Dove will generally go along with anything that sounds reasonable, especially if it is about buying something that enhances the home, or in some way makes things more comfortable for the family.

But if the purchase sounds extravagant, or unwarranted, the Dove will worry and fret and try to prevent the money being spent. "Do we really need it?"

If the Dove is married to another Dove, there is usually little drama when it comes to handling and spending money.

If the supportive Dove is married to the careful Owl, then the Owl will normally have the last say on where the money goes.

If the Dove is married to an Eagle, there are normally few problems on agreeing how their money should be spent.

If the Dove is married to a Peacock, ulcers for the Dove may well be on the cards!

Remember, Peacocks themselves don't get ulcers — they are just carriers!

THE EAGLE AND MONEY

The Eagle

"Money doesn't always buy happiness. People with ten million dollars are no happier than people with nine million dollars."

Remember, the Eagle is driven by the need for control and power. And that is just what money can buy them.

Eagles expect to live a better lifestyle than the rest of us and they normally do. What is more, they generally have little trouble financing it.

Whether their workaholic nature gives them time to really enjoy it, or not, is another matter.

While the Eagle likes to be in control of most things, they usually have little concern with domestic day-to-day expenses, or about how the money is spent.

In fact they usually 'don't want to know'. But when it comes to making decisions to spend a significant amount of money, it will be the Eagle who will generally have the last say.

If the Eagle is married to a Dove there is normally few hassles when it comes to spending money. The Eagle will make most of the decisions.

If the controlling Eagle is married to the cautious Owl there is real potential for conflict. The Eagle will want to spend on 'lifestyle', while the Owl will want to save.

If the Eagle is married to a Peacock they normally quite happily work out how to spend their money. The Eagle makes sure of that.

If the Eagle is married to another Eagle it can be a battle of the Titans if they happen to disagree about where the money should be spent. Ultimately though, they always work it out in the end.

THE OWL AND MONEY

The Owl

"You just can't have enough put away for a rainy day."

They say you can't take it with you, but many Owls give it a good try!

Remember, the Owl is driven by the need for predictability and security. And that is just what money can buy them.

The Owl is the most careful of all the styles when it comes to spending a dollar.

Spending money on 'non-essentials' (and there are a lots of non-essentials in the Owl's world) is like pulling eyeteeth.

Having said that, on the one hand the Owl can be penny-pinching in everyday things, then surprise everyone around them by buying the most expensive stereo, or home entertainment system, and the like.

If the Owl is married to another Owl, then there are usually few problems when it comes to spending money. Except on that stereo system!

If the cautious Owl is married to a supportive Dove, then it is normally the Owl who will have the last say on how and where the money should be spent.

If the Owl is married to an Eagle then there is a real potential for conflict. As mentioned before, the Eagle will want to spend on 'lifestyle', while the Owl will want to save.

If the careful Owl is married to a spendthrift Peacock it can create havoc (to say the least) when it comes to the question of spending money.

The Money Tree

It has been said that budgeting is a form of worrying before you spend instead of after.

Be that as it may, my daughters and their husbands swear by the family budgeting book *The Money Tree* written by a fellow Adelaide author.

If you are interested, the book is available by contacting the author, Diana Mathew, PO Box 501, North Adelaide, South Australia, 5006. Telephone 1800 686 008.

Diana, please send all commissions to the address at the front of this book!

It has been said, that marriage is the process of finding out what sort of partner your spouse would prefer!

14

THE FOUR BASIC STYLES IN A NUTSHELL

In the next section we'll get right up close and personal with the 16 personality style combinations.

But before we go on, let's wrap up where we've been so far.

THE FOUR BASIC STYLES IN A NUTSHELL

	PEACOCK *The Talker*	**DOVE** *The Feeler*	**EAGLE** *The Doer*	**OWL** *The Thinker*
OTHER NAMES	The Persuader The Actor The Promoter	The Supporter The Carer The Amiable	The Controller The Dominator The Enforcer	The Analyser The Thinker The Pessimist
WANTS	Popularity and fame	Belonging and friends	Authority and control	Order and predictability
MEASURES WORTH BY	Public Recognition	Warm Relationships	Quick Results	Systematic Accuracy
SEEN IN A NEGATIVE LIGHT	Loud Showy Superficial Talks too much	Unmotivated Soft Easily lead Oversensitive	Bossy Arrogant Pushy Impatient	Unsociable Picky Fussy Critical
COMMUNIC-ATION STYLE	Outspoken Unselfconscious Talks fast Expressive *They talk about themselves*	Softly spoken Self conscious Quiet Bashful *They ask about your wellbeing*	Strong voice Quick To the point Poor listener *They stick to business*	Softly spoken Self conscious Unemotional Detached *They give you all the fine details*
LOVES	Popularity	Acceptance	Winning	Certainty
HATES	Not being noticed	Rejection	Losing	Uncertainty
GOOD AS	Salespeople Entertainers Speakers	Team workers Carers Social workers	Project Leaders Military Leaders Union Leaders	Accountants Scientists Engineers

THE FOUR BASIC STYLES IN A NUTSHELL

	PEACOCK *The Talker*	DOVE *The Feeler*	EAGLE *The Doer*	OWL *The Thinker*
NOT GOOD AT	Analysing Emotional control Listening Punctuality	Being bossy Quick decisions Taking risks Being a loner	Tolerance Teamwork Diplomacy Being patient	Socialising Selling Quick decisions Taking risks
STRENGTHS	Persuasive Energetic Creative Optimistic	Compassionate Friendly Loyal Patient	Confident Decisive Independent Gets results	Careful Systematic Analytical Consistent
SHORT COMINGS	Undisciplined Talks too much Exaggerates Manipulative Self-centred	Unsure Dependant Over compliant Easily lead Possessive	Autocratic Unbending Undiplomatic Impatient Critical	Over-cautious Negative Indecisive Inflexible Self-righteous
OVERUSES	Showiness	Submissiveness	Bossiness	Conservatism
FEARS	Being just part of the crowd	Having to go it alone	Not being in control	Not having enough information
MOTIVATED BY	Recognition Applause Fame Adventure	Acceptance Approval Belonging Encouragement	Challenge Action Results Competition	Procedures Information Predictability Systems
REWARD WITH	Acknowledgement Compliments Praise	Reassurance Approval Acceptance Security	Challenge Freedom Status Authority	Security Predictability Structure Privacy

THE FOUR BASIC STYLES IN A NUTSHELL

	PEACOCK *The Talker*	**DOVE** *The Feeler*	**EAGLE** *The Doer*	**OWL** *The Thinker*
WHEN RELATING	Be quick Be friendly Let them talk	Go slow Be warm Be friendly	Be accurate Get to the point quickly	Go slow Be logical Be detailed
DEFENCE MECHANISM	Confronts Dramatic	Submits Quiet	Attacks Bossy	Withdraws Stubborn
UNDER PRESSURE	Becomes noisy then becomes friendly *"I was only joking"* **The Actor**	Becomes quiet then becomes stubborn *"We'll do what you want to do"* **The Martyr**	Becomes bossy then avoids or ignores *"My way or the highway"* **The Tyrant**	Becomes cooler and critical then withdraws *"I'm right and you're wrong"* **The Moralist**
CONFLICT STYLE	Problem solves *"Let's all be friends"*	Accommodates *"Let's keep the peace"*	Win/lose *"Winning isn't everything - it's the only thing"*	Avoids *"Do what you want to do but leave me out of it"*

15

UP CLOSE AND PERSONAL

Understanding ourselves, knowing what makes us tick, knowing what makes us different from other people, is the first step to personal progress.

Understanding others and what makes them different from ourselves, is the second.

In my opinion, these are the first two basic, but absolutely imperative, steps that need to be taken by anyone who is serious about forming a long lasting relationship.

UNDERSTANDING YOUR PARTNER'S WORLD

Empathy, as I have said before, is the ability to walk in another's shoes.

But we have to take our own off first.

Understanding and empathy gives us the opportunity to move into our partner's inner world. It helps us to see life as they see it.

Remember, when we understand each other, we can agree to disagree — without being disagreeable.

It has been said that understanding is not created — it is discovered.

I hope, that this section will offer you and your partner some signposts on the way to that discovery. It's time to take our shoes off.

ABOUT THE QUESTIONNAIRES THAT FOLLOW

On the following pages I have included 6 questionnaires:

- How I See Myself (For you to do on yourself)

- How My Partner Sees Me (For your partner to do on you)

- How I See Myself (For your partner to do on him or herself)

- How I see my Partner (For you to do on your partner)

- How My Friends See Me (For you)

- How My Friends See Me (For your partner)

If nothing else, it's been my experience with working with many hundreds of people that just by both of you doing the questionnaire, then comparing them with each other, can create an awful lot of lively and revealing discussion!

Questionnaires are always awkward to design, because words have different meanings to different people. Because of this, another way of finding your profile description is to read each of the profile descriptions and find the one that best describes you. If you see yourself in the description, then this is probably the one that best describes you.

HOW TO SCORE THE QUESTIONNAIRE

Add up all the ticks in each column to get totals.

Take the highest score as your primary style, and the next highest score as your secondary style.

For example, say you scored Peacock 8, Dove 14, Owl 11, Eagle 7, you would be described as a Dove-Owl.

If you have scored over 18 in one column and less than 6 in any other, then you should refer to the 'Extreme' description for that profile.

If it looks like you could be one, or another, read both descriptions and decide for yourself which one describes you best.

HOW I SEE MYSELF (FOR YOU)

Tick the words on the lists below which you think best describe you. Do not tick more than 40 or less than 20. And be honest with yourself. Then add up the number of ticks in each column.

☐ outgoing	☐ caring	☐ forceful	☐ conservative
☐ outspoken	☐ passive	☐ cool	☐ analytical
☐ enthusiastic	☐ calm	☐ independent	☐ practical
☐ motivating	☐ modest	☐ businesslike	☐ reliable
☐ optimistic	☐ gentle	☐ competitive	☐ quiet
☐ flamboyant	☐ sincere	☐ critical	☐ stable
☐ charming	☐ helpful	☐ assertive	☐ detached
☐ imaginative	☐ easygoing	☐ fast	☐ systematic
☐ persuasive	☐ even tempered	☐ decisive	☐ predictable
☐ unselfconscious	☐ pleasant	☐ self-reliant	☐ perfectionist
☐ carefree	☐ friendly	☐ bold	☐ reserved
☐ impulsive	☐ good listener	☐ bossy	☐ loner
☐ talkative	☐ shy	☐ impatient	☐ unemotional
☐ spontaneous	☐ sympathetic	☐ blunt	☐ pessimistic
☐ friendly	☐ supportive	☐ productive	☐ careful
☐ exaggerates	☐ trusting	☐ workaholic	☐ fussy
☐ animated	☐ dependable	☐ unbending	☐ stiff
☐ humorous	☐ kind	☐ decisive	☐ precise
☐ dramatic	☐ peaceful	☐ tough	☐ patient
☐ lively	☐ warm hearted	☐ determined	☐ diplomatic
☐ excitable	☐ intimate	☐ ambitious	☐ efficient
☐ energetic	☐ unassuming	☐ domineering	☐ restrained
☐ carefree	☐ sensitive	☐ strong-willed	☐ introverted
☐ entertaining	☐ co-operative	☐ aggressive	☐ indecisive

HOW MY PARTNER SEES ME

Tick the words on the lists below which you think best describes your partner. Do not tick more than 40 or less than 20. And be honest with him or her. Then add up the number of ticks in each column.

☐ outgoing	☐ caring	☐ forceful	☐ conservative
☐ outspoken	☐ passive	☐ cool	☐ analytical
☐ enthusiastic	☐ calm	☐ independent	☐ practical
☐ motivating	☐ modest	☐ businesslike	☐ reliable
☐ optimistic	☐ gentle	☐ competitive	☐ quiet
☐ flamboyant	☐ sincere	☐ critical	☐ stable
☐ charming	☐ helpful	☐ assertive	☐ detached
☐ imaginative	☐ easygoing	☐ fast	☐ systematic
☐ persuasive	☐ even tempered	☐ decisive	☐ predictable
☐ unselfconscious	☐ pleasant	☐ self-reliant	☐ perfectionist
☐ carefree	☐ friendly	☐ bold	☐ reserved
☐ impulsive	☐ good listener	☐ bossy	☐ loner
☐ talkative	☐ shy	☐ impatient	☐ unemotional
☐ spontaneous	☐ sympathetic	☐ blunt	☐ pessimistic
☐ friendly	☐ supportive	☐ productive	☐ careful
☐ exaggerates	☐ trusting	☐ workaholic	☐ fussy
☐ animated	☐ dependable	☐ unbending	☐ stiff
☐ humorous	☐ kind	☐ decisive	☐ precise
☐ dramatic	☐ peaceful	☐ tough	☐ patient
☐ lively	☐ warm hearted	☐ determined	☐ diplomatic
☐ excitable	☐ intimate	☐ ambitious	☐ efficient
☐ energetic	☐ unassuming	☐ domineering	☐ restrained
☐ carefree	☐ sensitive	☐ strong-willed	☐ introverted
☐ entertaining	☐ co-operative	☐ aggressive	☐ indecisive

HOW I SEE MYSELF (FOR YOUR PARTNER)

Tick the words on the lists below which you think best describe you. Do not tick more than 40 or less than 20. And be honest with yourself. Then add up the number of ticks in each column.

☐ outgoing	☐ caring	☐ forceful	☐ conservative
☐ outspoken	☐ passive	☐ cool	☐ analytical
☐ enthusiastic	☐ calm	☐ independent	☐ practical
☐ motivating	☐ modest	☐ businesslike	☐ reliable
☐ optimistic	☐ gentle	☐ competitive	☐ quiet
☐ flamboyant	☐ sincere	☐ critical	☐ stable
☐ charming	☐ helpful	☐ assertive	☐ detached
☐ imaginative	☐ easygoing	☐ fast	☐ systematic
☐ persuasive	☐ even tempered	☐ decisive	☐ predictable
☐ unselfconscious	☐ pleasant	☐ self-reliant	☐ perfectionist
☐ carefree	☐ friendly	☐ bold	☐ reserved
☐ impulsive	☐ good listener	☐ bossy	☐ loner
☐ talkative	☐ shy	☐ impatient	☐ unemotional
☐ spontaneous	☐ sympathetic	☐ blunt	☐ pessimistic
☐ friendly	☐ supportive	☐ productive	☐ careful
☐ exaggerates	☐ trusting	☐ workaholic	☐ fussy
☐ animated	☐ dependable	☐ unbending	☐ stiff
☐ humorous	☐ kind	☐ decisive	☐ precise
☐ dramatic	☐ peaceful	☐ tough	☐ patient
☐ lively	☐ warm hearted	☐ determined	☐ diplomatic
☐ excitable	☐ intimate	☐ ambitious	☐ efficient
☐ energetic	☐ unassuming	☐ domineering	☐ restrained
☐ carefree	☐ sensitive	☐ strong-willed	☐ introverted
☐ entertaining	☐ co-operative	☐ aggressive	☐ indecisive

HOW I SEE MY PARTNER (FOR YOU)

Tick the words on the lists below which you think best describes your partner. Do not tick more than 40 or less than 20. And be honest with him or her. Then add up the number of ticks in each column.

☐ outgoing	☐ caring	☐ forceful	☐ conservative
☐ outspoken	☐ passive	☐ cool	☐ analytical
☐ enthusiastic	☐ calm	☐ independent	☐ practical
☐ motivating	☐ modest	☐ businesslike	☐ reliable
☐ optimistic	☐ gentle	☐ competitive	☐ quiet
☐ flamboyant	☐ sincere	☐ critical	☐ stable
☐ charming	☐ helpful	☐ assertive	☐ detached
☐ imaginative	☐ easygoing	☐ fast	☐ systematic
☐ persuasive	☐ even tempered	☐ decisive	☐ predictable
☐ unselfconscious	☐ pleasant	☐ self-reliant	☐ perfectionist
☐ carefree	☐ friendly	☐ bold	☐ reserved
☐ impulsive	☐ good listener	☐ bossy	☐ loner
☐ talkative	☐ shy	☐ impatient	☐ unemotional
☐ spontaneous	☐ sympathetic	☐ blunt	☐ pessimistic
☐ friendly	☐ supportive	☐ productive	☐ careful
☐ exaggerates	☐ trusting	☐ workaholic	☐ fussy
☐ animated	☐ dependable	☐ unbending	☐ stiff
☐ humorous	☐ kind	☐ decisive	☐ precise
☐ dramatic	☐ peaceful	☐ tough	☐ patient
☐ lively	☐ warm hearted	☐ determined	☐ diplomatic
☐ excitable	☐ intimate	☐ ambitious	☐ efficient
☐ energetic	☐ unassuming	☐ domineering	☐ restrained
☐ carefree	☐ sensitive	☐ strong-willed	☐ introverted
☐ entertaining	☐ co-operative	☐ aggressive	☐ indecisive

HOW MY FRIENDS SEE ME (FOR YOU)

Tick the words on the lists below which you think best describe you. Do not tick more than 40 or less than 20. And be honest with me — I can take it!

☐ outgoing	☐ caring	☐ forceful	☐ conservative
☐ outspoken	☐ passive	☐ cool	☐ analytical
☐ enthusiastic	☐ calm	☐ independent	☐ practical
☐ motivating	☐ modest	☐ businesslike	☐ reliable
☐ optimistic	☐ gentle	☐ competitive	☐ quiet
☐ flamboyant	☐ sincere	☐ critical	☐ stable
☐ charming	☐ helpful	☐ assertive	☐ detached
☐ imaginative	☐ easygoing	☐ fast	☐ systematic
☐ persuasive	☐ even tempered	☐ decisive	☐ predictable
☐ unselfconscious	☐ pleasant	☐ self-reliant	☐ perfectionist
☐ carefree	☐ friendly	☐ bold	☐ reserved
☐ impulsive	☐ good listener	☐ bossy	☐ loner
☐ talkative	☐ shy	☐ impatient	☐ unemotional
☐ spontaneous	☐ sympathetic	☐ blunt	☐ pessimistic
☐ friendly	☐ supportive	☐ productive	☐ careful
☐ exaggerates	☐ trusting	☐ workaholic	☐ fussy
☐ animated	☐ dependable	☐ unbending	☐ stiff
☐ humorous	☐ kind	☐ decisive	☐ precise
☐ dramatic	☐ peaceful	☐ tough	☐ patient
☐ lively	☐ warm hearted	☐ determined	☐ diplomatic
☐ excitable	☐ intimate	☐ ambitious	☐ efficient
☐ energetic	☐ unassuming	☐ domineering	☐ restrained
☐ carefree	☐ sensitive	☐ strong-willed	☐ introverted
☐ entertaining	☐ co-operative	☐ aggressive	☐ indecisive

HOW MY FRIENDS SEE ME (FOR YOUR PARTNER)

Tick the words on the lists below which you think best describe you. Do not tick more than 40 or less than 20. And be honest with me — I can take it!

☐ outgoing	☐ caring	☐ forceful	☐ conservative
☐ outspoken	☐ passive	☐ cool	☐ analytical
☐ enthusiastic	☐ calm	☐ independent	☐ practical
☐ motivating	☐ modest	☐ businesslike	☐ reliable
☐ optimistic	☐ gentle	☐ competitive	☐ quiet
☐ flamboyant	☐ sincere	☐ critical	☐ stable
☐ charming	☐ helpful	☐ assertive	☐ detached
☐ imaginative	☐ easygoing	☐ fast	☐ systematic
☐ persuasive	☐ even tempered	☐ decisive	☐ predictable
☐ unselfconscious	☐ pleasant	☐ self-reliant	☐ perfectionist
☐ carefree	☐ friendly	☐ bold	☐ reserved
☐ impulsive	☐ good listener	☐ bossy	☐ loner
☐ talkative	☐ shy	☐ impatient	☐ unemotional
☐ spontaneous	☐ sympathetic	☐ blunt	☐ pessimistic
☐ friendly	☐ supportive	☐ productive	☐ careful
☐ exaggerates	☐ trusting	☐ workaholic	☐ fussy
☐ animated	☐ dependable	☐ unbending	☐ stiff
☐ humorous	☐ kind	☐ decisive	☐ precise
☐ dramatic	☐ peaceful	☐ tough	☐ patient
☐ lively	☐ warm hearted	☐ determined	☐ diplomatic
☐ excitable	☐ intimate	☐ ambitious	☐ efficient
☐ energetic	☐ unassuming	☐ domineering	☐ restrained
☐ carefree	☐ sensitive	☐ strong-willed	☐ introverted
☐ entertaining	☐ co-operative	☐ aggressive	☐ indecisive

ABOUT THE PROFILE DESCRIPTIONS

The following profile descriptions are meant to help us to understand the differences between our partners and ourselves, to understand and appreciate that we have different preferences for the way we think, feel and act.

Of course the world forces us to be different people at different times. We act the part we are supposed to play. But being human, we will always want to return to our comfort zones, to being our natural selves. You can only act a part for so long.

And even while acting the part, we are still driven by the values and beliefs which drive our natural style.

A GUIDE TO THE GALAXY

Keep in mind that we are all unique. None of us share the same fingerprints, nor do we fit neatly into boxes. Descriptions of personality styles are simply a guide to the galaxy of human nature. They are like a road map – a guide to the terrain. And like any map, they don't show the beauty and complexity of the country itself, in this case, the complexity and beauty that makes us unique individuals.

EIGHT OUT OF TEN AIN'T BAD

All questionnaires and descriptions of human nature have their limitations; this one is no different. If after completing the following questionnaire, and then reading your profile description, you feel that around 80 per cent of the description describes you fairly accurately, then this is probably the preferred style that you feel most comfortable with when operating with the world.

16

THE 16 PARTNER STYLES

The following section contains descriptions of the 16 different combinations of the personality styles, along with some tips for living with them.

QUICK INDEX TO THE 16 PARTNER STYLES

The Extreme Peacock Partner	166
The Peacock-Dove Partner	175
The Peacock-Eagle Partner	183
The Peacock-Owl Partner	190
The Extreme Dove Partner	195
The Dove-Peacock Partner	202
The Dove-Eagle Partner	209
The Dove-Owl Partner	214
The Extreme Eagle Partner	220
The Eagle-Peacock Partner	227
The Eagle-Dove Partner	235
The Eagle-Owl Partner	240
The Extreme Owl Partner	247
The Owl-Peacock Partner	253
The Owl-Dove Partner	258
The Owl-Eagle Partner	264

*Everybody's beautiful
in their own way.*

THE EXTREME PEACOCK PARTNER

"Come on, let's have some fun. You take life far too seriously. We're here for a good time, not a long time — so let's go for it!"

"Yeah, that might be OK for you, but there are some things that do need to be taken seriously."

"Yeah? Name one."

So speaks the Extreme Peacock expressing the guiding philosophy of all Extreme Peacocks — life is for living, so enjoy it while you can.

You'll know an Extreme Peacock when you meet one — you can't miss them! Happy-go-lucky, cheerful, easygoing and confident in any company, (and usually the centre of attention) they are talkative and extremely friendly. They can be great company.

They are jovial and naturally funny people who are accepting of others and are the friendliest and outgoing of all the personality styles. They always know the latest joke and can't wait to tell it, whether you want to hear it or not!

The Extreme Peacock personality style is also known as the entertainer, the performer, the actor, and the exhibitionist. They'll join in eagerly to anything that looks like a bit of fun. They are the original party animal and see themselves as (and can be) the life of any party.

They love an audience, the bigger the better. Wherever there's a spotlight you'll find an Extreme Peacock basking in its glow. Their need for drama, to be the centre of attention, and to perform, is almost an addiction. Hollywood is the home of many Extreme Peacocks.

They love making people happy. Generous to a fault, they get a great deal of pleasure out of giving. And quite often they will give when they really can't afford to.

The Extreme Peacock talks louder, and certainly laughs more and louder than most other people. Their body language is fast and expressive, and usually quite dramatic. They use lots of facial expressions and sweeping hand gestures. They know all the latest 'in-words' and phrases and use them often. One of their favourite past-times is talking about themselves. Their conversations contain a lot of "I" and "Me" words.

They know what's going on, especially about 'who's doing what' socially.

First-class name-droppers, they like to let you know how many important people they know.

They are great storytellers who never let the facts get in the way of a good story, especially if stretching the truth can get them out of a tight spot. In other words, they can have a tendency to 'handle the truth carelessly'. As natural actors they can play any part the situation calls for, and then convincingly deliver the lines required. To an Extreme Peacock, words only have meanings for the moment.

Just about everything they do is 'over the top'. They are great believers in 'if a little bit is good, then a lot must be better'. Whether it's perfume, after-shave, ointment, jewellery — especially the chunky gold stuff — you name it, they like lots of it. And they can be a bit the same way when it comes to things that aren't so good for them too, like smoking, drinking, over-eating and the like. In other words, they can be addictive when it comes to things they like, which is a lot of things!

They like to have 'nice things' around them. Appearance and image is very important. How others see them means a lot to the Extreme Peacock. Their dress can be quite flamboyant. They like to keep up with the fashions and dress stylishly. They love bold and bright colours, especially red, which is often the colour of their car, which usually has custom number plates. As they get older, cosmetic surgery is often on the agenda.

Impulsive, excitable and always on the move, they are hard to keep up with. And they are good at getting other people caught up in their ideas. But generally their excitement doesn't last too long as they tend to jump from one thing to another. They are good starters, but not so good as finishers. They simply lose interest when 'sameness' creeps in and things start to get repetitive — which to the Extreme Peacock means 'boring' — which is one of their greatest hates. How some people do the same things day after day is a total mystery to them. They like changing situations. They want to be where the action is.

Extreme Peacocks are the original 'Cockeyed Optimists' who genuinely believe that things will work out for them, so they don't worry about things too much, particularly about being on time, or about spending money, which they often get into trouble with. "How you can save money and have all the good things in life?" is another mystery to them.

Drama is a constant life theme.

Extreme Peacocks are the 'Drama Queens' and 'Drama Kings' of the world. Almost everything they do is done with a theatrical flourish. They are always on stage. Both joy and tragedy seem to stalk them. Everything that happens to them is magnified by ten compared to the rest of us. A normal life seems boring compared to theirs. Nothing that happens to them is ever 'ordinary'. It is always extreme. When they are up they feel 'absolutely fantastic', and when they are sick they are 'dying'.

In a nutshell

Extreme Peacocks love the joy of living, and they are the best of the styles when it comes to enjoying the 'now moment' and going along with whatever comes. They are optimistic, impulsive and carefree, they want life to be fun — it's a game — it shouldn't be taken too seriously. Life is an adventure that should be filled with excitement. They are generous and share what they have with loved ones and strangers alike. They are sensitive to other people's feelings, especially other's suffering. They are exceptionally kind to others and have a special affinity to children and animals. Like a playful puppy, they are free and fun loving, but will want to move on if things get too boring, or if they feel there's a tight collar and a short leash about to be put on them.

Word portrait

Confident, friendly, outgoing, expressive, gregarious, playful, talkative, charming, enthusiastic, energetic, easygoing, excitable, impulsive, adventurous, boisterous, daring, sociable, adaptable, considerate, outspoken, cocky, optimistic, flamboyant, imaginative, persuasive, unselfconscious, carefree, spontaneous, animated, humorous, dramatic, lively, entertaining, good-hearted.

Wants

Wants lots of attention, approval, affection, reassurance and compliments. They want to be noticed and in the spotlight. They want to be popular and admired by others. How they look to others is extremely important, hence their need for status symbols.

Admires

They admire people who are imaginative, are quick thinkers, and who have good verbal skills. They especially admire achievers with a public profile who also have these qualities.

Influences

They influence others with their friendliness, infectious enthusiasm and their optimism, as well as their confidence, humour, and verbal skills.

Strengths

People-orientated. Fun loving, invigorating, enthusiastic and optimistic. Good verbal skills. Can persuade and motivate others. Imaginative, thinks in broad concepts, generates ideas. A confident risk taker — will take on challenges.

Shortcomings

- Highly emotional and sensitive — takes everything personally.

- Undisciplined when it comes to time. To say punctuality is not one of their strengths is an understatement.

- Generally disorganised. They dislike doing detailed or analytical things, especially having to do paperwork, or family budgets, or sticking to them. They can also tend to jump from one thing to another without finishing the first.

- Because of their natural enthusiasm and willingness to please, they often take on more than they can handle, resulting in delivering less than they promised.

- Can become excitable, impatient and manipulative when what they are not getting what they want.

- Because recognition, applause and status symbols are important to them, they will go into debt (sometimes heavy debt) to 'look good'.

- They dislike being alone. They need constant company.

- They are rarely, if ever, self-critical. They can be experts at shifting blame. They have a natural skill for being able to move the blame on to others, or blame 'bad luck', for anything bad that may happen to them, or for any shortcomings they may have.

- Because of their impulsiveness, coupled with their sense of fun and adventure, they can be outrageous flirts.

- They can be seen (especially by the Owl types), as self-centred, exhibitionist, a show-off, boastful, intrusive, loud, over-sensitive, unreliable, loose with the truth, vague and scattered. And their constant enthusiasm can be tiring.

How they communicate

Extreme Peacocks gain energy talking, and lose it listening, which is why they like talking and not listening. Listening for any length of time (like about 18 seconds) is like digging holes to the Extreme Peacock — it's exhausting — it's just too hard for them.

When they talk, they tend to speak without thinking. It's out before they've given it any thought. They speak quickly in a torrent of words that are full of emotion, and with a dramatic touch — sometimes with a highly dramatic touch. They speak in colourful phrases and use similes, examples and word pictures, and they use their hands to gesture with dramatic flourishes.

They like the conversation to be centred on themselves. They like to talk about what they've been doing, how they feel — not on what you've been doing, or how you feel. Their conversations are 'me' centred.

Under pressure

Anger is never very far from the surface for an Extreme Peacock, especially when they're under pressure. They have a very short fuse. Under pressure the Extreme Peacock will fly off the handle with lots of emotion, noise and drama. They become explosive, volatile and loud, and they personalise their attacks using strong emotional language. Once they've got it off their chest, they quickly cool down and usually (too quickly for some) want to be friends again. Peacocks fight first and become friendly quickly after.

Under pressure they are prone to exaggerate and bend the truth to get them out of trouble.

Fears

Permanence or sameness — being locked into repetitious routines and situations.

Basic Instinct

They are driven by the need for public applause and personal admiration.

Turn Ons

- Being in the spotlight.
- Praise and admiration.
- Performing.
- Being popular.
- Having fun.
- Parties.
- Adventurous sex.
- Telling jokes and stories.
- Making people happy.
- Spending money.
- Knowing important people.
- Looking good to the outside world.
- Having nice clothes and surroundings.
- Flashy cars and jewellery.
- Fast-moving situations.
- Being imaginatively creative.
- Talking about themselves.
- Over-indulging (in almost anything).
- Being told how good they are (at anything).
- Winning awards (especially an Oscar!).

Turn Offs

- Being stuck in an unchanging situation.
- Being bored.
- Being alone.
- Being ignored or overlooked.
- Being taken for a sucker.
- Having to be patient.
- Listening.
- Waiting in queues.
- Reading instruction manuals.
- Being 'ordinary'.
- Staying home.

Common bad feelings

Anger and envy.

Living with the Extreme Peacock

Living with an Extreme Peacock can be like living in a Hollywood movie. Impulsive, hooked on change, full of fun and excitement, one thing is for sure, life will never be dull, you won't be wanting for a bit of drama and excitement. That's when they're up, that is. Because when they're down, they can be really down. Fortunately though, they have more ups than downs.

If marriage is contemplated, then being married while parachuting, or abseiling down a mountain, or the like, may well be on the cards, and forget a honeymoon in a nice relaxing spot, because that will be seen as deadly boring.

Peacocks are (or like to think they are) sexy. They are the most sexually playful and adventurous of all the types. They love to experiment. They love talking about it. They love hearing about it. But most of all they love doing it. Their sexual experiments can be very adventurous, to say the least. (Or so they say!)

You are going to have to accept that your partner is excitable, impulsive and spontaneous in both their actions and decisions, sometimes dramatically so. They tend to say just what they think without really thinking about it, and this can cause some fairly serious frustration for partners who think a little more deeply.

Remember also that the Extreme Peacock lives by the principle of; 'If it feels good — do it', and will sometimes jump in feet first and get their (and your) toes burned doing it. This is especially true for going into debt to look good.

After a while of living together, Extreme Peacocks can quite often disillusion their partners, because they rarely live up to their romanticised image. Their partners often discover that 'what you see is not always what you get'.

In a close relationship, the Extreme Peacock can become a tenacious Pygmalion sculpture that chisels away at their partner in an (always futile) attempt to shape them into an image of themselves. "Don't be so boring" is one of their sharpest chisels.

As a parent, the Extreme Peacock highly values their personal freedom, so it's only natural that they want to give that same freedom to their children. But they don't normally let them abuse the privilege. They encourage their kids to test themselves, to do things on their own as soon as possible, to be free spirits, so that they can fly from the nest as soon as they're ready.

Many of the more 'serious styles' enjoy their exhilarating company — for a while. But ultimately when the relationship gets serious they will try to tame them. That's when the Peacock can start to feel trapped and look for a way out as gracefully as possible, or get out in any way possible.

They like to take one day at a time and find it difficult to commit to a long-term relationship. Have fun, play the field — "Why lock yourself in?" But when they're ready to settle down they're easy to get along with and will put up with all sorts of nagging and criticism — which usually acts like water off a duck's back. But if there's too much of it the Peacock might well spend more and more time away from home.

Their partners invariably have major problems with them when it comes to money. As far as the Peacock is concerned money is to be enjoyed, not saved. The latest 'toy' always beckons. They don't do this with any nasty intent, they just want to enjoy it now — "You could be dead tomorrow." They also spend money on friends, or even just acquaintances. Even when next to broke, they will pick up the bill at a restaurant to 'look good' which can really cause some hassles on the home front.

When the 'error of their ways' is pointed out to them (which by the way, they don't see as errors), they will do their best to 'reform' and try to live up to their promises with the best of intentions, but it's normally fairly short-lived. "I just can't help myself."

A relationship with an Extreme Peacock can be exciting and fun and never boring. They see it as their mission to give pleasure and excitement to their mates. But a word of caution: A relationship between two Extreme Peacocks can be fairly unstable and often doesn't last very long. Hollywood proves this.

But if you are prepared to let your Extreme Peacock partner have centre stage and the freedom to perform, and give them the applause and acknowledgment that they so desperately need (you have to tell them you love them about every five minutes, it keeps them breathing — it's their oxygen), and just enjoy the show, rather than criticise them (which some partners tend to do, which is absolute poison to the Extreme Peacock), there will be more highs than lows in the relationship.

If you're looking for a serious and steady stay-at-home partner, you may think twice about getting involved with an Extreme Peacock. But if you like a bit of risk and excitement and have a sense of drama and adventure, then put your seat belt on and hang on for the ride, because things will never be dull. That's for sure.

THE PEACOCK-DOVE PARTNER

"Don't try to understand me, because I'm different. I'm an original. I express myself using my artistic talents."

So speaks the Peacock-Dove expressing the guiding philosophy of all Peacock-Doves. Deep down they believe they are (and have a need to be) special. They can't stand being ordinary. They want to be different and they want you to notice it.

They have a strong need to express themselves and to be seen as original. They have a natural eye for beauty and can express their feelings in dance, music, painting, the theatre, or literature. Many become artists, musicians, poets and playwrights.

Often referred to as the 'Romantics', they are imaginative, intuitive, and creative and are often actors, musicians, songwriters, fashion designers and the like who have a natural talent for blending words, colours, textures and sounds.

If not involved in arts, or crafts, or music, they will invariably have some other form of creative expression in their lives. They will totally immerse themselves in it, often taking on menial jobs for financial support until they 'make it' in their chosen artistic field.

They enjoy being eccentric. It can be orange hair, studs in their noses and eyebrows, obvious tattoos, or their clothes, (they would never wear anything that is plain or average — it has to be different). It might be their flamboyant and theatrical behaviour, or it may well be all of the above. Peacock-Doves set out to be noticed, to be different and to do whatever it takes to accomplish it.

The entertainment business, the arts, and the fashion industry are their natural habitats. Hollywood is a magnet to them. Look on the cover of TV Week and you will invariably see a Peacock-Dove face smiling out.

On the one hand they have a playful joy for living. To the Peacock-Dove life is for pleasure, they want to have fun — and they can put on the most creative and imaginative (and sometimes the craziest) parties you've ever been to. On the other hand they often feel lonely and fear being abandoned. They can experience dark moods of emptiness and despair with feelings of not being deserving of love.

They can expect too much of themselves and long for what they don't have. This combination of feelings can lead to envy and jealousy about what others may have. They can become quite obsessive over resentments — they carry a good grudge.

Warm and compassionate with a keen interest in other people, they are the creators (they write the words to our love songs) and the performers of the world. They love to impress and long to perform — to put on a show. Easygoing, friendly and talkative, they are usually good fun to be with. They are sensitive and compassionate and are also the most excitable of all the personality types. They can go from being highly excited one minute, to being bored out of their minds the next.

They are the kids who were bored to death at school. They were restless, talked a lot in class, and couldn't wait to leave. Except for perhaps sports, art and music, they saw little at school that would be of any use to them. School systems are just not designed for the imaginative and impulsive Peacock-Doves.

Supremely optimistic, they always feel lucky. Daring, bold and adventurous, they will take risks just for the thrill of it. And if it doesn't work out, "Oh, well, better luck next time." And they rarely look back. "Tomorrow is another day."

Like a playful puppy, they are free and fun loving, and they will quickly move on if there is a hint of a tight collar, or a short leash, about to be put on them. They hate being told what to do and can become rebellious and do just the opposite. Self-discipline is certainly not one of their strengths.

Because they can quickly become bored, they are not particularly good at staying in one place, or doing the same thing. They hate doing routine ("boring!") things, and if forced, they will somehow vary them, and turn them into an interesting and fun activity.

Easygoing and very approachable, they are people-people. Kind and generous to a fault, (Elvis Presley gave away Cadillac cars) they get a great deal of pleasure out of giving. They are also sympathetic and tactful with a willing ear for other people's problems.

They have great faith in their intuition and rely on their impulses to guide them. They have little use for rules and regulations. If rules are forced upon them they will bend them. Instinctive and intuitive, they quite often put faith in horoscope predictions, psychic readings and the like, and may feel themselves gifted with certain metaphysical powers of prediction.

Emotionally restless, their lives are often spent 'trying to find themselves'. ("Who am I? Why am I here?"). And in a search for the 'proper way'. Some experiment with different philosophies and religions and with what others may see as 'way out' ideas. Many are vegetarians, animal rights activists, feminists and adherents to unusual ideas about health.

They are highly sensitive to other people's feelings, especially to other's suffering. They are exceptionally kind people with a special affinity to children and animals. They often have jobs (or would like to have) that bring them into contact with children and animals.

They are go-getters who earnestly go after what they set out for — and usually achieve it. Many of our musicians, singers, writers and actors are Peacock-Doves who have come from obscurity to become famous and popular through 'hanging on in there'.

Quite often scandalous or forbidden behaviour seems to fascinate them. Hire and watch the movie 'Iris'. It is a true story based on the life of Iris Murdoch, an Oxford philosopher and successful novelist, (and a Peacock-Dove) who was married to John Bayley, an Oxford professor, (and an Owl-Dove) for 40-odd interesting years. Not only is it a great story (and a real tear-jerker), but also both actors play their parts to perfection and give a real insight into the characters of a Peacock-Dove and an Owl-Dove. Interestingly enough, as was this one, relationships between these two styles are usually highly successful.

In a nutshell

Peacock-Doves are optimistic, witty, active, and impulsive. They are creative, artistic and spontaneous. They live in the now moment, not much caring about the past. What's done is done. They are rarely preoccupied with the future. Tomorrow is another day. Enjoying life is their first objective. Freedom to act on impulse is their oxygen of life. Warm, trusting and understanding, they are people-people who make lovable friends and partners.

Word portrait

Fun loving, outgoing, outspoken, enthusiastic, energetic, kind, friendly, impressive, excitable, sensitive, impulsive, creative, artistic, dramatic, adventurous, lively, mobile, daring, promoting, playful, optimistic, charming, flamboyant, imaginative, persuasive, sensual, unselfconscious, carefree, talkative, spontaneous, exaggerates, animated, humorous, entertaining, considerate, forgiving, tactful, tolerant, adaptable, generous, easygoing, scattered, over-reliant.

Wants

To be different, to be creative, to have fun.

Admires

They admire creative people who have 'made it'.

Influences

They influence others through their creativity, their friendly and pleasant nature and sense of child-like fun.

Strengths

Creativity and sensitivity.

Shortcomings

- Can be self-absorbed, moody and envious of others.

- Highly emotional and sensitive — takes everything personally.

- Can become excitable, impatient and manipulative when not getting what they want.

- They dislike being alone. They need constant company.

- Undisciplined when it comes to time and generally disorganised. They dislike doing detailed or analytical things, especially paperwork, or family budgets. They can also quickly jump from one thing to another without finishing the first.

- They are rarely, if ever, self-critical. They can be experts at shifting blame. They have a natural skill for being able to move the blame on to others, or blame 'bad luck', for anything bad that may happen to them, or for any shortcomings they may have.

- They can be seen (especially by the Owl types), as self-centred, over-sensitive, unreliable, vague and scattered.

How they communicate

They are askers, not tellers. They beat around the bush when they want something.

When they talk, they tend to speak without thinking. It's out before they've given it any thought. They speak quickly in a torrent of words that are full of emotion, and with a dramatic touch — sometimes with a highly dramatic touch. They speak in colourful phrases and use similes, examples and word pictures, and they use their hands to gesture with dramatic flourishes.

They like the conversation to be centred on themselves. They like to talk about what they've been doing, how they feel — not on what you've been doing, or how you feel. Their conversations are 'me' centred.

Under pressure

Under pressure they become emotional and moody in order to manipulate the outcome they want.

Because they're so sensitive, they often lump together 'who they are' with 'what they do', and can therefore interpret criticism of something they've done as a personal attack. This can cause them to be offended very easily. On the other hand, they respond warmly to compliments and praise for a job well done.

Fears

Being ordinary.

Basic Instinct
They are driven by the need to be different.

Turn Ons

- To be different — to stand out from the crowd.
- To express themselves in some artistic way
- To put on a show.
- Public praise and personal admiration.
- To have fun.
- Parties.
- Changing situations.
- Taking creative risks.
- Adventurous sex.

Turn Offs

- Being 'ordinary'.
- Criticism of any sort.
- Not being noticed.
- Being ignored or overlooked.
- Being alone.
- Listening.
- Having to read an instruction manual.
- Being locked in to a boring routine.
- Being told what to do.
- Rules and regulations.
- Staying home.

Common bad feelings
Envy, anger and depression (dark moods).

Living with the Peacock-Dove Partner
On a good day, the Peacock-Dove can be a generous, openhearted, sensitive and loving partner. Their usual cheerful nature can bring humour and good times to any partnership. Sexually adventurous, they make great lovers who like to experiment in all sorts of creative ways!

On a bad day (or three), they can have complicated and dramatic mood shifts. They can become depressed and be quite moody for days and even weeks, and there are times when their partners wonder what the 'score' is as they suffer the hot-and-cold treatment. One minute they can't live with you, the next they can't live without you. Their dark moods can also involve temper tantrums accompanied with biting criticism. All this can be used as levers to manipulate their partner into getting what they want.

In their dark moods they focus on what is wrong with them rather than what is right with them. They often feel like an outsider, different and isolated. A constant search for their 'true self' often preoccupies them, which can be a little wearing on a partner who is comfortable in their own skin.

Highly emotional, they are sensitive to the slightest critical remark. They can blow what others say out of all proportion. They get upset very easily.

They often long for what they don't have and are often envious of others. Any interest (no matter how innocent) by their partner in someone else can often turn to fierce jealousy. It's pointless to tell them that they are oversensitive and overreacting, because they already know that.

As a parent, they are usually good with their children, supporting and encouraging their creativity and originality. Because the Peacock-Dove values their personal freedom, it's only natural that they want it for their children, but they don't let them abuse the privilege. They encourage their kids to test themselves, to do things on their own as soon as possible, to be free spirits, so that they can fly from the nest as soon as they're ready.

As mentioned before, Peacock-Doves are often attracted to their opposites, the Owl types and this can be a mutually rewarding relationship. The Owl type being conservative and grounded offers stability to the Peacock-Dove, while at the same time, the Peacock-Dove brings a little light-heartedness and humour to the relationship, which can result in a nice balance for both.

To summarise; in a relationship the Peacock-Dove is self-revealing, supportive, gentle, playful, passionate and witty. They can also be self-absorbed, jealous, emotionally child-like, moody and overly critical.

They get hurt and feel rejected easily. They tend to think that the grass is greener on the other side and can get down and depressed about it. When down they can become very needy of your constant attention and time. All this can become very draining if they're relying on only you for their emotional needs and support.

The Peacock-Dove is a sensual lover and a romantic. If you're willing to tread softly when it comes to stepping on their sensitive toes, give them lots and lots of compliments and tell them you love them very often, then you couldn't go past a Peacock-Dove for a loving and caring partner. One thing is for sure; you will never be bored or looking for something to do.

THE PEACOCK-EAGLE PARTNER

"Life is an exciting adventure, or it's nothing."

Helen Keller originally said it, but it could be the anthem of all Peacock-Eagles. They crave for excitement and they'll go out of their way to find it. They need changing situations, stimulation and new experiences. They are adventurers and adrenaline addicts. They enjoy life to the hilt.

Enthusiastic and energetic, they go through life with heroic optimism. They believe they are invincible. Risk-takers, adventurers and gamblers, they always see the glass as half full.

They are socially confident, outgoing, talkative, witty and charming, but rather than being over the top, (like the Extreme Peacock), they are tougher of mind. They find it hard to make a commitment to a career and are generally not an expert in any one thing, but seem to do many things well.

They are at ease in groups. They like people, and people usually like them. They see humour in a situation more quickly than others. Chatterboxes and good storytellers, they are happy people with a childlike, cheerful and infectious sense of humour. When others are unhappy they get them to lighten up and see the bright side. If you need cheering up, call a Peacock-Eagle friend.

They love a laugh and will often play the clown role. Wisecrackers, and joke tellers, their appetite for jokes and humour never let up. Unfortunately this sometimes leads to them being seen as immature and may not be taken seriously enough by the more serious personality types.

They like themselves and are good to themselves. Cockeyed optimists and positive thinkers, they rationalise negatives ("Don't worry about it, things will get better.") Some say that they wear rose-coloured glasses believing that positive thinking will solve all life's problems. And they rarely blame themselves for anything bad that befalls them. ("It really wasn't my fault, what happened was..."). They quickly let go of grudges and grievances and recover from loss faster than most people.

They love to travel, because travel offers them the things they yearn for — change, excitement, adventure and pleasure.

Always busy, they usually have several irons in the fire at once. They do things in high spurts of energy and activity, often juggling many things at once. They are good starters, but not so good as finishers, especially if finishing means doing something repetitious, because they hate being locked into a set routine. ("It's boring!") Rather, they thrive on excitement, change, challenge, variety and fast moving situations.

Of all the styles, the Peacock-Eagle is the most charming and persuasive. They can also be the most manipulative. They can operate on people with amazing skill and charm and are often referred to as the 'Promoter' or the 'Casanova-type'. They could sell ice to the Eskimos — or win any heart.

They are extremely good at promoting themselves, their ideas, or anything else they believe in. Their natural talents often lead them into leadership positions, selling, acting, politics and the like.

While just as impulsive and excitable as the other Peacocks, the Peacock-Eagle is more competitive and ambitious by nature. Shrewd and aggressive, they want to be the top dog and will do and say whatever it takes to get there. They want victory. While the other Peacocks play for the sake of play, the Peacock-Eagle plays to win.

They exaggerate everything. More is better. Whether it's telling stories, eating, drinking, working, more projects, more recognition, more possessions, more fun, more joy, more pleasure. Prone to addiction, they just can't get enough of what turns them on.

Crafty and highly resourceful, they are the most artful of all the Peacocks. They have an uncanny ability to inspire confidence and have all the natural skills and theatrical flair needed to succeed in almost anything they care to take on. Witty, charming and cocksure, they excel as politicians, entrepreneurs, negotiators, salespeople, swindlers, racketeers and con artists. They live by their wits.

They deal in hunches, ideas and intuition. They remember faces and forget names.

Chameleon-like, they can be whatever you want them to be. They are good at sensing what form of attention or flattery appeals to others — and using it. They are name-droppers, wear fashionable clothes, especially designer labels, and are always out to impress others. They want to make an impact.

They can be the masters and mistresses of the sudden whirlwind courtship; the sudden irresistible infatuation accompanied by extravagant gifts and exaggerated romantic gestures. ("I love you Tracy" written in the sky).

Like all Peacocks, they like 'nice things' around them. Impressive homes, gold chunky jewellery and flashy cars, (usually red with custom number plates), are big on their agenda, and they will go into debt to buy these and other 'toys' in order to look good to the outside world — because looking good is very important to the Peacock-Eagle. As they get older, plastic surgery may well be on their agenda.

Needless to say, they are not good at managing money. Money to the Peacock-Eagle is for enjoying, not for saving. "You might be dead tomorrow, so enjoy it while you can."

Even when broke, they'll pick up the bill at a restaurant to look good. ("Let me handle this.") When the credit card bill comes in it often causes a bit of stress on the home front, especially if their partner is careful at handling money. If their partner is another Peacock type they are forever juggling money and may well have a dozen different credit cards with most of them up to their limit.

Outgoing and charming, and often physically attractive, they can be terrible flirts in search of a conquest. But once the conquest has been achieved they move on to greener pastures, or return to their 'normal pasture'.

The Peacock-Eagle is often portrayed in books and movies as a con artist, and very often as a scoundrel and a cad — or all three wrapped up in one. Both Michael Caine and Steve Martin play a classic portrayal of the charming and manipulative Peacock-Eagle in the movie "Dirty Rotten Scoundrels". Nicole Kidman also plays a Peacock-Eagle to perfection in the movie, "To Die For". Both of these movies are worth a look.

In a nutshell

Peacock-Eagles are optimistic, witty, energetic and enthusiastic with an ability to gain the respect and confidence of all types of people. Trusting and self-assured, they inspire enthusiasm and goodwill. They are actively dominant and assertive. Because of this, they tend to win positions of authority, prestige and status, which is an important driving force to them. They are adventurers and risk-takers who love accomplishing a challenge and especially the 'applause' that goes with it. They influence others through their openness, warmth, charm and persuasive manner.

Word portrait

Confident, good humoured, enthusiastic, playful, uninhibited, articulate, animated, charming, romantic, witty, smooth, persuasive, outspoken, ambitious, daring, go-getter, self-promoter, talkative, gift of the gab, joke-teller, adventurous, flamboyant, fun loving, entertaining, humorous, optimistic, energetic, opportunistic, manipulative, excitable, impulsive, self-centred, restless, dramatic, boastful, aggressive, argumentative, self-absorbed, scheming, crafty.

Wants

To be famous.

Admires

Those who have made it on their wits and talent.

Influences

They influence others through their warmth, charm and persuasive manner.

Strengths

Enthusiasm, optimism, warmth and persuasive abilities.

Shortcomings

- Can be over-optimistic, especially about their ability to motivate and influence those who don't want to be.

- They tend to become restless and fidgety when not challenged or in the spotlight.

- Can tend to come on too strong at times.

- Can use their charms to manipulate.

How they communicate

They are tellers, not askers. Good talkers and terrible listeners.

They say just what's on their mind and it often gets them into trouble.

Articulate, expressive and persuasive, they communicate using animated facial expressions and talk in colourful language, with dramatic body language and gestures delivered with theatrical flair to add emphasis to what they're saying.

Peacock-Eagles can tend to 'stretch the truth'. They have a tendency to say whatever it takes to convincingly persuade and get their way. Like all Peacocks, they are natural actors and can play any part the situation calls for. Sometimes, their words only have meanings for the moment.

Under pressure

They have difficulty dealing with emotional problems, and will avoid them wherever possible. They begin fooling around and telling jokes when things get tight.

Hypersensitive to criticism, they will push it aside with a smile and a few witty remarks, but deep inside it hurts.

If the pressure gets too 'heavy' they attack with plenty of dramatic noise and emotion. But once the storm is over they cool down quickly and want to become friends again.

They don't hold a grudge. They don't look back. They get on with life ("Let's move on.") and expect everybody else to do the same.

Fears

Being locked into a routine with no challenges or adventure, or any opportunity to use their imagination and persuasive skills.

Basic Instinct

They are driven by the need for public recognition and status symbols. They want to be famous.

Turn Ons

- Achievement/Winning.
- Praise and admiration.
- Status symbols (of any kind).
- Changing situations.
- Risk and adventure.
- Travel.
- Being generous.
- Telling jokes and stories.

- Making people happy.
- Persuading others.
- Being romantic.
- Doing many things at once.
- Knowing important people.
- Looking good to the world.
- Parties.
- Adventurous sex.

Turn Offs

- Not being recognised or applauded for their talents.
- Criticism of any sort.
- Listening.
- Being ignored or overlooked.
- Being locked into a routine.
- Being taken for a sucker — to be conned.
- Having to be patient.
- Listening.
- Waiting in queues.
- Reading instruction manuals.
- Being 'ordinary'.
- Staying home.

Common bad feelings

Anger and worry.

Living with the Peacock-Eagle

Peacock-Eagles are warm, generous, witty, good humoured, romantic, and generally good fun to be with.

They can also be manipulative. They are skilled at using both intimate and subtle tactics, or straight out aggression in an attempt to mould their loved ones into a personal vision of who they want them to be. They can be serious Pygmalion Chiselers.

When they are up, they are really up, and fortunately they are up more than they're down. But when they are down they are really down. There is no in between for the Peacock-Eagle — it's up or down. And their downs are accompanied with moods of dark depression. When this happens, they need a lot of encouragement and moral support from their partner to get them back on track.

When squeezed into a corner, they become emotional and dramatic with very sharp and loud tongues. Then just as quickly (too quickly for most people) they cool off and want to become friends and lovers again. The up side to this is that they don't hold a grudge. "What's done is done."

They are exciting and fun-loving partners who want the freedom to do their 'own thing'. And they tend to move on if they start to feel the pressure of a tight collar or short leash about to be put on them.

Like all Peacocks, Peacock-Eagles are (or like to think they are) sexy. They love talking about it. They love hearing about it. But most of all they love doing it. They are sexually playful and adventurous. They love to experiment. And their sexual experiments can be very adventurous, to say the least. (Or so they say!)

When locked into a boring situation they become restless, fidgety, cranky and irritable. When bored, they will create some sort of excitement or drama in their lives. When this happens at home, it may take the form of provoking some sort of conflict in order to get a rise out of a less emotional partner. For the partner of a more settled nature this can be a real pain in the bum.

As a parent, because the Peacock-Eagle highly values their personal freedom, it's only natural that they want the same freedom for their children. But they don't let them abuse the privilege. They encourage their kids to test themselves, to do things on their own as soon as possible, to be free spirits, so that they can fly from the nest as soon as their ready.

Marriage to a Peacock-Eagle can be exciting and fun, and never boring. They see it as their mission to give pleasure and excitement to their mates. But a word of caution: A relationship between two Peacocks can tend to be unstable and doesn't last very long. Hollywood proves this.

Chameleon-like, the partners of Peacock-Eagles often have a hard time knowing just whom they are dealing with. But if you keep in mind that image and status — the symbols of success — are right on the top of their personal agenda, and if it fits in with your values, and you're willing to support him or her in that quest, then you're in for an exciting and interesting ride.

THE PEACOCK-OWL PARTNER

"Flaming enthusiasm, backed up by horse sense and persistence, is the quality that most frequently makes for success."

Dale Carnegie originally said it, but it could well be the anthem of all Peacock-Owls.

Peacock-Owls are poised, socially confident and self-assured with an unruffled calm about them. They can be witty and charming and have a natural ability to involve those around them to help get what they want.

They are optimistic and calculated risk takers who are confident of their own talents. They have the ability to take creative ideas and apply them to practical uses.

They are imaginative and creative as well as logical and practical people who have a high drive factor to win at whatever they take on. They like a bit of danger and the thrill of conquering it. They strive for, and usually get, what they go after.

They have a natural ability to win others to their point of view using emotional appeal as well as facts and logic. Those who do not think as fast as the Peacock-Owl can often feel over-powered by their force of logical persuasion.

Although friendly and sociable, the Peacock-Owl can also be a cool, quiet onlooker, seeming to observe and analyse life with a detached curiosity one minute, and the next, can surprise everyone with a flash of original humour by making some quick witty comment.

They are pragmatic people. They like to get the job done in the easiest and most practical way while still staying popular with those around them. Being popular is important to the Peacock-Owl. It's almost as important to them as the freedom to do their own thing. Almost.

They like social approval as well as being recognised for their natural skills and abilities. Because of this they often seek positions of leadership and thrive on the prestige that goes with it — they want to be the Top Dog — and be recognised and applauded for it.

Gifted with great eye-hand coordination, they are absolute naturals at using tools and implements of almost any sort, including brushes, sculpture chisels, scalpels and especially 'sporting tools'.

They are usually interested in how and why things work. If they become interested in a particular field, they will completely immerse themselves, becoming almost inspired, and then attack it with a passion to the exclusion of almost anything else.

Being adept with all sorts of tools, they are also gifted with a natural eye for line, colour, form and graceful composition. They instinctively see how all the parts fit and blend perfectly (and beautifully) together. They take pride in having this ability which often leads them into creative fields like architecture, painting, sculpture, arts and crafts, or similar creative pursuits that allows them to use their natural talents.

They also tend to move with a certain gracefulness — with an almost ballet-like coordination. Watch a smooth-flowing champion golfer take his or her shot, or a champion surfer in action, and you will see the natural graceful physical movements of a Peacock-Owl on display.

They like a challenge and they work at a fast pace. They tend to work in spurts of high energy. Many find it difficult to keep up with them. When this happens, the Peacock-Owl tends to lack tolerance and often becomes impatient and critical.

Excitable, spontaneous and impulsive, they trust their impulses and instincts. They become restless quickly and lose interest in situations that lack competition and challenge. They like to be where the action is. The Peacock-Owl likes to organise the parade, then lead it. Once the parade is over, they will look for another one.

Peacock-Owls like to follow their own rules. They want to be free to follow their instincts and creativity. They have little time or respect, for authority and other people's rules, rarely allowing them to get in their way to prevent them doing their own thing.

In a nutshell

Peacock-Owls are self-starters, fast paced, competitive, witty and can be fun to be with, while at the same time they are logical and analytical in their search for the most direct way of getting results. They want to lead the field in whatever interests them and will do so with a passion. They want to be the Top Dog. More than any other type, Peacock-Owls love action more than pleasure. They are driven to do their own thing with a passionate pride in their natural skills and abilities. They seek victory and triumph in whatever they take on.

Word portrait

Confident, sociable, energetic, talkative, optimistic, enthusiastic, persuasive, diplomatic, adventurous, lucid, perceptive, imaginative, outspoken, sensible, adaptable, pragmatic, detailed, logical, objective, precise, fussy, obsessive, impatient, argumentative, intolerant.

Wants

The freedom to do their own thing.

Admires

They admire people who initiate action. People who get things done against all odds.

Influences

They influence others through their fast pace and their natural creativity.

Strengths

Imagination and creativity balanced with a logical and practical approach.

Shortcomings

- Gets bored and fidgety quickly.

- When bored, looks for a way out, and usually finds it.

How they communicate

They usually tell, not ask.

Generally softly spoken, they prefer to communicate through action, rather than using verbal skills. Their conversation is usually to the point.

Under pressure

Under pressure, the Peacock-Owl becomes restless, impatient and critical. They can be quick to attack.

Fears
Boredom. Being restricted. Being trapped in mundane routine.

Basic Instinct
They are driven by the need to do their own thing They want action with results.

Turn Ons

- Challenge and Achievement.
- Public praise and personal admiration.
- Changing and stimulating situations.
- Action and adventure.
- Taking calculated risks.
- Using their creative imagination and talents.
- Putting ideas into practical use.
- Leading others.
- Being popular.

Turn Offs

- Unchanging and non-challenging situations.
- Rules and regulations.
- Slow-moving people.
- Not being recognised or applauded for their talents.
- Criticism of any sort.
- Being told what to do.
- Being 'ordinary'.
- Staying home.

Common bad feelings
Boredom.

Living with the Peacock-Owl
Peacock-Owls can be unpredictable and hard to get to know. On one hand, they can be outgoing and fiercely loyal and generous to their

friends and partners. On the other hand they can be loners who try at all costs to avoid being 'locked in'.

Peacock-Owls need their freedom. It pays to give them plenty of rope. A short leash will only drive them away.

The Peacock-Owl will try at all costs to escape routine and boredom. They generally seek some form of recreational excitement with a thrill, a dare, or a risk in it, and they will take off and do it on impulse, at any time, just because they feel like it. They thrive on excitement. Because of this, they can have a tendency to go off with their friends for extended lengths of time taking time out from the family.

Naturally gifted artists, sculptures and artisans, they can also be skilful Pygmalion Sculptors who psychologically chisel away at their mates in an effort to make them 'perfect' — to shape them to their vision. And they can do this with a vengeance.

Marriage to a Peacock-Owl can be exciting and fun, and never boring. They see it as their mission to give pleasure and excitement to their mates. But a word of caution: A relationship between two Peacocks can tend to be unstable and doesn't last very long. Hollywood proves this.

As a parent, because the Peacock-Owl highly values their personal freedom, it's only natural that they want the same freedom for their children. But they don't let them abuse the privilege. They encourage their kids to test themselves, to do things on their own as soon as possible, to be free spirits, so that they can fly from the nest as soon as their ready.

So, if you're looking for a free spirit to share your life with, and are prepared to spend some time alone, then the Peacock-Owl may be the right partner for you.

THE EXTREME DOVE PARTNER

"We're put on this earth to help each other, well that's what I believe, anyway."

This is an Extreme Dove expressing the guiding philosophy of all Extreme Doves — that people are the most important thing in the world and that we should all care for each other.

If the world was full of Extreme Doves there would never be another war. Calm, humble, gentle and peace-loving people, they hate to see suffering of any sort. Considerate, warm, soft and gentle, they are the most sensitive and compassionate of all the personality styles.

Throughout most of history, society has presumed that women are (or should be) Doves and they have generally been portrayed as such. But nothing could be further from the truth because there are as many male Doves in the world as there are female Eagles. Being a Dove, or an Eagle, is not a gender thing.

Self-conscious and painfully shy socially, Extreme Doves can sometimes appear to others as distant. They are introverted and quiet people who are seldom outwardly jovial or playful and always strictly follow socially acceptable standards of behaviour.

Extreme Doves were the most well behaved students at school. They were the kids that never put a foot wrong. As adults they still follow that pattern and rarely, if ever, make their presence felt. Placid, quiet and even-tempered, there are times when you wouldn't know the Extreme Dove was there — which they are quite happy about — the last thing they want is to make their presence felt. Being the focus of attention is acutely embarrassing to them.

Extreme Doves want you to love them, or at least like them. If you don't, then the last thing they want is for you to tell them. They hate conflict or ill feeling of any kind. (That's if they hate anything at all) and see anger as a character weakness and try to hold it back at all cost.

They tend to label people as their 'friends' rather quickly, and are proud that so many people pour their hearts out to them. Pleasant and friendly, they look for the good in people. ("Even criminals have a good side.") They are good listeners with a willing and sympathetic ear for whatever ails you. Caring, supportive, and easy to get on with, they make good friends and loyal, loving and devoted partners.

Given a willing ear, Extreme Doves will tell you their life story at the drop of a hat, particularly if it's a sad story, as many seem to be. Perhaps this is because their kind, gentle and caring nature is often taken advantage of by less sensitive partners, or ex-partners.

Extreme Doves find a sense of security in dealing with people and situations they are familiar with. They don't like change or disruptions to their normal pattern of doing things and they like to stay in the same place, whether in a home, or a job.

They are the 'Really nice people who will do anything for you'. Except sell anything — that would be pushy. Extreme Doves are never pushy, but ask them to help in the canteen, or a busy bee and they will be the first there.

Always anxious that they might make a mistake, they try to avoid anything that sounds risky. And they don't like to have things thrown at them suddenly. They need a lot of warning. They need to plan ahead, cover all the bases before they can relax, and even then they will continually keep going over the 'What Ifs?' in their mind.

Trying always to please and over-apologetic, they often start their conversations with the word "Sorry". It's as if they use it as an 'insurance policy' in case they offend someone later. In fact, the Extreme Dove spends a lot of time apologising — mostly for things that are not their fault.

Plagued with low self-esteem (which is the foundation of confidence), Extreme Doves constantly self-examine and question themselves. What self-esteem they have comes more from *what* they can do to help others, rather than from *who* they are as a person.

The Extreme Dove is like a deer — always on the alert, tentative and acutely aware of what's going on around them. And like the deer, they become startled and nervous if caught in the public headlights. Hypersensitive, especially to criticism, the Extreme Dove is quick to tears. Tense and nervous, they are often afraid of the world, feeling vulnerable and out of place, like strangers in a strange land. They are afraid of letting go, of losing themselves in any experience. Although internally emotional, outwardly their faces remain placid and show little, if any, outward feeling for the moment.

Because they are so sensitive and empathetic, they can 'over-empathise'. It's as if they actually feel the emotional experiences of others. In a sickroom, for instance, where others are suffering, they can get so 'over-empathetic' that they become distressed to the point of giddiness, or actual fainting.

They are givers and helpers who will give you 'the last shirt off their back'. When they hear the words, "I need you" they melt. They can't say "no." They will do almost anything for you, even though they may later regret it. ("Why in the Hell did I say I'd do that?"). Or if they promised more than they could deliver, they'll feel guilty as well as irritated.

Extreme Doves are fully capable of unusual sacrifices for what, or who, they believe in. History shows them as long-suffering, self-sacrificing martyrs — often as saints.

In a nutshell

Calm, warm, loving, patient and tolerant, Extreme Doves make loyal, supportive, and dependable friends and partners. Peaceful and gentle, they are the 'Carers of the World'. Hypersensitive and shy, they keep themselves to themselves. They like the company of close friends and loved ones — things they're familiar with — and will go out of their way to avoid strangers and strange (and to them threatening) social situations. Easy to live with, they are solid and sensible people who avoid risks and don't give their partners any sudden surprises.

Word portrait

Calm, considerate, shy, caring, patient, tactful, friendly, passive, tolerant, diplomatic, compassionate, solitary, deep, detached, adaptable, easygoing, loyal, flexible discreet, modest, gentle, sincere, helpful, tranquil, pleasant, even-tempered, good listener, sympathetic, supportive, trusting, dependable, kind, peaceful, warm hearted, unassuming, sensitive, co-operative, hypersensitive, inhibited, withdrawn, intuitive, unrealistic, evasive, vague, procrastinating, scattered.

Wants

Wants the security of dealing with non-threatening people and familiar situations.

Admires
Loyalty, humility, and evenness of mood and temperament.

Influences
They influence others through their gentle nature and their dependability and loyalty.

Strengths
Supportive. Reliable. Loyal. Predictable. Even-tempered.

Shortcomings

- Over-sensitive.

- Not good in unpredictable situations.

- Reacts poorly to change.

- Their innate 'over-humility' and deep-rooted lack of confidence ("What if I make a mistake?") can prevent them from accomplishing all they are capable of.

How they communicate
Slower paced and relaxed, they are friendly and non-threatening. They are good listeners with lots of eye contact and attentive smiles and nods. They show interest through mirroring the facial expressions of those they're conversing with.

Extreme Doves are askers, not tellers. They do not force their opinions or values on others. Non-assertive, when they want something, they will beat around the bush rather than coming right out and asking for it.

Under pressure
They are hypersensitive towards criticism. Any criticism can pull the rug from under their feet. In a group, it may take only one person to make a

critical comment about them for them to think, "Everybody's against me!"

When the Extreme Dove is threatened or put under pressure they withdraw into themselves and away from the person or situation that is causing the discomfort. They become submissive and pliable. If offended, or put out, they tend to suffer in silence. Under attack the Extreme Dove takes flight.

In fearful or critical situations, the Extreme Dove can become confused and immobilised (they freeze). Their emotional circuits seem to overload and short out, especially when it comes to an emotional experience of conflict and hurt.

Under the stress of having to do something that they do not agree with, they do a 'slow burn' and play the 'mute withdrawal game'.

Fears

They fear being rejected.

Basic Instinct

They are driven by the need to be accepted and loved.

Turn Ons

- Being needed.
- Helping, caring and supporting others.
- Staying in the background.
- Sticking to the rules.
- Familiar people and situations.
- Doing one thing at a time.
- Family.
- Staying home.

Turn Offs

- Rejection (of any sort).
- Conflict.
- Criticism (of any sort).
- Being put in the spotlight.
- Unfamiliar situations.
- Taking risks.
- Sudden changes.
- Telling people what to do.

- Dealing with difficult people.
- Being forced to do many things at once.
- Parties with strangers.
- Not being able to say "No."
- Being alone.

Common bad feelings

Fear and anxiety.

Living with the Extreme Dove

'Steady as she goes' would be a good description of living with an Extreme Dove, because they live by the principle of, 'Don't rock the boat — even if it's heading for the rocks'.

They are the Homemakers. Home is where the heart is.

They can do the same thing day after day, year after year, without seeming to get bored.

Mild-mannered, quiet and even-tempered, when everyone around them is laughing out loud at something funny, they will be quietly smiling. The Extreme Dove is never loud — at anything.

Their calm, even, and predictable nature can be comforting and reassuring, and their distaste for conflict and arguments ensures that peace reigns. But having said that, their closed-off nature and tentativeness in not wanting to talk things out can be frustrating to the more outwardly emotional and expressive personality styles.

Their 'lack of initiative' can also be a source of annoyance to the more assertive personality styles such as the Peacocks and the Eagles. If they want things to happen, they find themselves making most of the decisions — and taking most of the action to get it done.

Don't expect your Extreme Dove partner to gush over you with loving words of endearment, or expect too many spontaneous hugs and kisses. That's not their style. Although serious and faithful in their love, they can seem distant and aloof in expressing their affection, either verbally or physically. And they can often have a deep-seated fear of sexuality which is perhaps partly a fear being sexually inadequate.

Although quiet, calm and compassionate, they can never the less, like the rest of us, be capable Pygmalion chisellers who play the game of 'Why can't you be more like me?' They do this in their own quiet way, but with just as much effect as the 'louder' verbal personality styles.

Once committed to a relationship, they make their loved one, and the relationship, the centre of their world. They live for the relationship, and can live their life through their partner. They are intuitive and extremely sensitive to the moods of their mates. Like litmus paper, if their partner is happy, so are they. If their partner is unhappy, so are they. How their partner feels at the time is how the Extreme Dove feels.

Natural nurturers, as parents they love their children unconditionally. They are warm and encouraging, or suffer guilt if they aren't. They can tend to worry excessively about their kids and can become fiercely (over) protective.

If you don't expect your partner to be outwardly emotional, and are happy that they want to live a peaceful quiet life at home without the need for too many parties, or spring too many surprises on you, then the Extreme Dove is your ideal partner.

In a nutshell, the Extreme Dove is loving and lovable. If you are looking for a quiet, loving, and loyal partner, then the Extreme Dove will be your partner for life — literally. Doves mate for life.

THE DOVE-PEACOCK PARTNER

"That's just me. What you see is what you get. I don't put on airs and graces, or make out to be somebody I'm not. I can't stand people who do that."

So speaks the Dove-Peacock. They strive to be 'authentic' and true to themselves and to others. It is important to them. The Dove-Peacock doesn't try to put on an act, or wear a mask.

At first glance the Dove-Peacock can be mistaken for a Peacock. Effervescent and friendly, they have an honest open face and a warm smile.

Everybody loves the Dove-Peacock. Almost always cheerful and enthusiastic, they are good with people and fun to be around. Sensitive, warm and caring, they are also invariably popular and admired for their willing and sympathetic ear for whatever ails you.

The Dove-Peacock's feelings are close to the surface and easily aroused. They are hardly able to keep quiet about their thoughts and feelings. As kids they began to talk early, and to their parents they never seemed to stop. Their school report cards always mentioned their 'talkativeness and inability to concentrate'.

They are openhearted people who radiate personal warmth and sincerity and have a natural talent for relating intimately with people. They look for the good in others and generally find it. They are caring and supportive of others and make people feel both wanted and needed.

With an almost sixth sense (hypersensitive), they are constantly tuned in to how other people are feeling. When other people are happy, so are they. When others become upset, so do they.

They hate conflict and disharmony of any sort and will do anything in their power to avoid it. Because of this, they will always try to fit in, thereby avoiding conflict — and rejection — which is their second hate.

With a desperate need to please (almost everyone), Dove-Peacocks have a hard time saying "No." This often sees them sacrificing their own time and needs as they beaver away doing favours for just about anybody who asks. With little strength of willpower with others, they also find it hard to say "No" to themselves. "I just can't help myself." They are often 'emotional eaters' and many have weight problems as a result.

Extremely adaptable, Dove-Peacocks are steady and reliable people who generally do things in an accepted and approved pattern. They prefer to take a low profile in most situations, particularly with assertive (especially aggressive) people, yet they can be fiercely assertive, independent and stubborn when something, or someone, they believe in is threatened.

Friendly and easygoing, they prefer to be one of the team rather than being the leader and having to make the hard (and unpopular) decisions. Never the less, they can be quite independent and self sufficient when it comes to getting a job done, and relied on to do it right.

'Doing the right thing' is extremely important to them. They can develop a fierce and loyal commitment to people, organisations, and causes that are important to them, as well as becoming ardent and vocal advocates for reform. Many of our protesters and the people who work for Greenpeace, and the like, are Dove-Peacocks.

High spirited and highly imaginative, they seek new experiences and are open to all of life's possibilities. They can't bear to miss out on what's going on around them. As good communicators, they want to spread the word. They do this on a one-to-one basis, or as a journalist, writer, documentary filmmaker, playwright, or in any other form that lets them tell of their experiences. Deep down they seek an ideal world and do their bit to make it happen.

Dove-Peacocks are often called the 'Romantics.' They have a highly romantic imagination and are people of strong passions. They are the most spontaneous of all the Doves. They open up their hearts and share their feelings — they wear their hearts close to their sleeves. And the male Dove-Peacock is the most caring and chivalrous of all the personality styles when it comes to his relations with women.

When dating, Dove-Peacocks rarely play the field; rather, they prefer to go out with one person at a time. Romantic and idealistic, they seek the perfect mate — the love of their life. They want a match made in heaven. Generally they would rather just sit and talk with their dates than do things or go places. At a party, the Dove-Peacock will invariably be with his or her date in a corner talking.

Most Dove-Peacocks find their greatest satisfaction is in organising most of their lives around their home and families. Sentimental to the core, they love their friends and family around them — or not too far away.

They are usually imaginative and creative around the house. Their homes are usually filled with music, family photographs, books, flowers, (Dove-Peacocks love their garden and flowers) and 'artistic' or 'crafty' things they have made. There is usually a musical instrument somewhere — which they can actually play. And when visiting, whether announced or not, you will always feel warmly welcome in their home.

In a nutshell
Dove-Peacocks are sincere, warm, openhearted people who are ferociously loyal to the people and causes that are important to them. Romantic and sentimental, particularly about their friends and family, they make caring and supportive friends and partners and kind and nurturing parents.

Word portrait
Friendly, open, expressive, enthusiastic, sociable, sensitive, polite, considerate, intuitive, perceptive, dedicated, compassionate, imaginative, tender, considerate, trusting, cooperative, accepting, devoted, tactful, diplomatic, adaptable, easygoing, flexible, appreciative, altruistic, idealistic, empathic, sympathetic, ethical, hypersensitive, romantic, sentimental, excitable, unrealistic.

Wants
To be needed. To please. To be accepted by others.

Admires
People who are steady, loyal and dependable — people who 'do the right thing.'

Influences
They influence others through their openness, kindness, sincerity and loyalty.

Strengths
Caring, friendly, loyal, compassionate, trusting and supportive.

Shortcomings

- Over-idealistic.

- Tends to be too kind and trusting.

- Needs to be more careful of those who want to take advantage of their good nature.

How they communicate

Warm, friendly and talkative, they talk with animated expressions and body language.

They are both good talkers, as well as good listeners — a rare ability!

They are askers, rather than tellers. "If you get time, would you please ....." "If it's not too much trouble could you please ...?"

Rather than telling, they give information, ask questions, make suggestions; "Have you ever thought that we could ...?"

Under pressure

The Dove-Peacock generally appears cheerful, unruffled and unconcerned, even under stress. But inside there can be a storm going on.

If put under pressure, they tend to become compliant and adaptable. They can say 'yes' but they really mean 'no'.

Under the stress of being forced to do something they don't agree with, they'll have their say, do a slow burn and play the 'silent game.' This silent treatment works well for them, because they can show their disapproval without the need to argue. Because of their friendly nature, and need for harmony, these moods don't last long. Of all the personality types, the Dove-Peacock is the champion of the principle of 'Forgive and forget.'

In fearful or critical situations, they can become confused, flustered and immobilised (they freeze). Their emotional circuits seem to overload and short out, especially when it comes to an emotional experience of conflict and hurt.

Because they are so sensitive, they can also tend to 'over-empathise.' It's as if they're actually feeling the emotional experiences of others. In a sickroom, for instance, where others are suffering, they can get so 'over-empathetic' that they can become distressed to the point of giddiness, or actual fainting.

Fears
Disharmony. Aggressive people and conflict situations.

Basic Instinct
They are driven by the need to 'do the right thing'.

Turn Ons

- Being needed.
- Helping, caring and supporting others.
- Approval and praise — especially "I love you."
- Being true to themselves.
- Being friendly and popular.
- Doing the 'right thing' by people.
- Gatherings of family and friends.
- Music.
- Gardening and/or craftwork.
- A happy home.

Turn Offs

- Rejection.
- Criticism (of any sort).
- Conflict or disharmony.
- Being taken for granted.
- Telling people what to do.
- Missing out on 'what's happening'.
- Can't say "No" to others.
- Can't say "No" to themselves.

Common bad feelings
Anger and anxiety.

Living with the Dove-Peacock

Dove-Peacocks make kind, warm, loving and devoted partners. They are generally totally committed to their loved ones to whom they show deep affection and caring, and they will bend over backwards to maintain harmony.

Because of their romantic nature, and because they seek the perfect mate, they can more often than not project an idealised image on to their loved one. As a result, they are more likely than most personality styles to be blinded to their partner's flaws, leading them to believe that they have found their perfect mate and that they will live 'happily ever after'.

When reality kicks in, ("You're not who I thought you were.") and their partners show themselves to be as human as the rest of us, with just as many faults, they can often attempt to make their loved ones live up to their idealised image. This is when the Pygmalion Chisels and sandpaper come out. And like all sandpapering, it can cause quite a bit of friction.

While they are totally committed, protective and dedicated to their loved ones, they are also totally committed to 'reforming' them. Remember, they are driven by the need to 'do the right thing' and they expect their partner to do the same. When they suspect their partner has 'gone off the rails', the sound of Pygmalion chisels chipping away may be heard.

As they grow in confidence in the relationship, they tend to seek a certain amount of independence and space to do their own thing. This may well take the form of some creative pursuit, or working within the community. It pays to give them this space.

Dove-Peacocks are loving and caring. Expressing their love and affection by giving hugs and kisses and saying "I love you" is as natural as breathing to them. But, if their partner begins to seem weak and clingy, needing more and more attention and appreciation, they can become irritable, insisting unexpectedly that their mate stops needing their approval and starts making their own decisions. It pays their mate to stand on their own two feet.

They like novelty, variety, and people in their lives. They can become restless and bored if they have to face the 'same old people and situations'. They also like the company of others, and are good at getting people together, especially family and friends.

In a parental role, Dove-Peacocks although totally devoted to their children, can be unpredictable in handling them. They can shift quickly from being a 'friend' one minute, to being a stern boss the next. While they may express strong opinions about discipline, when it comes to the crunch, they generally leave it to their mate to follow through fearing that they might lose the 'friendship' of their children. Their partners need to be prepared to be the disciplinarian.

No matter how many years they've been together, they still love a romantic dinner out with their partner — or better still the odd romantic weekend getaway to keep the romance alive.

Thoughtful of others, they rarely, if ever, forget birthdays or anniversaries. And the quickest way to hurt them is to forget theirs. It pays their partner to keep a diary!

Dove-Peacocks are a source of continuing protection, love and support to their partners. If you are looking for a devoted partner, and are willing to do the 'right thing' by them, then you couldn't go past the cheerful, warm and loving Dove-Peacock.

THE DOVE-EAGLE PARTNER

"To thine own self be true."

Dove-Eagles echo Shakespeare's words when they express their rule for living, which is, "Don't try to be anybody but yourself." Being authentic to themselves and others is a guiding life principle. They don't put on airs and graces, or pretend to be anybody they're not.

They have a relaxed layback style about them. Nothing seems to ruffle them. They are quietly and modestly confident of who they are and what they can do. They have no need for pretension, or cheers from the crowd.

Like all Doves, the Dove-Eagle is friendly, modest and rather bashful in public. But unlike the other Doves, the Eagle characteristics in their personality make them quite competitive, goal-orientated and quietly confident of their abilities. Underneath their modest exterior beats a highly competitive heart.

The happy mix of the Dove and the Eagle in their make up also makes them quite charming giving them a certain charisma. They are popular — people like and admire them and want to be around them. In sport they are gracious in losing, and even more gracious in winning.

Bright and cheerful, they are often referred to by their friends as 'lovely, generous and easygoing people', but as previously mentioned, beneath their placid and peaceful exterior is a fiercely driven person with clearly defined and driving goals bent on succeeding at whatever challenge they choose to take on.

They are people who think for themselves and care about others. They have a deep conscience and often involve themselves in humanitarian pursuits.

They were the kids the other kids followed. They always seemed to have interesting things for the group to do and just assumed a natural, but unassuming, leadership role which the 'team' was happy to follow. The same thing happens quite naturally in their adult life. They manage to take charge without seeming to, while those around them support them and work eagerly to help them.

They are interested in people — in human nature — in what makes people tick. They love to 'people watch' and read other people for their personalities. And they love books like this one! They trust their intuition, especially their natural intuitive skill for reading people, and rarely are they wrong about their insights into other people's motives and intentions, both good and bad. But they are extremely tolerant and rarely critical of others. Eagle-Doves look for the good in people, and usually find it, and believe we should all do the same. In fact, one of their pet hates is people who are prejudiced.

Dove-Eagles value relationships and harmony and handle people with charm and concern. They are invariably popular wherever they are. Good communicators, they are usually good with language and often find jobs as teachers, lecturers, counsellors, journalist, in the media, the clergy, in fact anywhere their natural talents for dealing with people and spreading positive messages and information can be used.

Interested in the growth and development of others, they consider people to be number one. Because of this, others often turn to them with their problems knowing that they'll get their understanding and support. This can often see them over-extending themselves both emotionally, and in time, on other people's problems or needs, sometimes to the detriment of their own relationships.

Trusting, optimistic, hopeful and enthusiastic, they are the masters and mistresses of seeing the positive side of things — both in people and life situations.

Robin Williams in the role of the teacher in the movie 'Dead Poet's Society' displays the classic characteristics of the Dove-Eagle to perfection: Natural charisma, independent thinking, a talent for using language, a caring attitude, plus an enthusiasm for the self-development and personal growth of others.

In a nutshell

'Just be yourself and think for yourself' is a guiding value and the Dove-Eagle's rule for living. Being authentic to themselves and others is a driving force. They don't put on airs and graces, or pretend to be anybody they're not. They are bright, cheerful and optimistic people with an even temper. People are attracted to them because of their personal integrity, their bashful charm and their caring nature. They are generous and look for, and generally see, the good in people. They are dedicated to spreading goodwill and enlightening others, especially about the 'deeper values' of life.

Word portrait

Relaxed, charming, gregarious, enthusiastic, quietly competitive, trustworthy, popular, caring, gentle, affectionate, optimistic, sociable, diplomatic, responsible, sensitive, idealistic, sympathetic, intuitive, imaginative, accepting, adaptable, ingenious, insightful, appreciative, considerate, tactful, efficient, responsible, independent.

Wants

To spread goodwill and help those around them to 'grow'.

Admires

People who are sincere and show compassion for others.

Influences

They influence others through their compassionate and caring attitude.

Strengths

Cheerful, optimistic, even-tempered, compassionate, independent thinker.

Shortcomings

- Their idealistic view of the world (or what it should be) can get in the way of reality.

- The heart can make too many decisions for the head.

- Inclined to project an idealised (perfect) image onto their loved one that is impossible to live up to.

How they communicate

They will tend to tell, rather than ask or suggest. But this is invariably done diplomatically and tactfully with a view to helping.

Under pressure

Normally calm and unruffled in almost any situation, the Dove-Eagles rarely loose their cool. (Which can drive the more expressive styles nuts!) Conflict is painful to them and they will do whatever is needed to avoid it. They seek a quiet, harmonious and peaceful life.

Fears

Conflict and disharmony.

Basic Instinct

They are driven by the need to enlighten and educate others.

Turn Ons

- Winning (quietly).
- Being true to themselves — doing their 'own thing'.
- Enlightening and helping others
- Harmonious relationships.
- People who look for the good in others.

Turn Offs

- People who are insincere and phoney.
- People who are negative or prejudiced.

Common bad feelings

Worry — but not often.

Living with the Dove-Eagle

Dove-Eagles seek to fall in love once — and for a lifetime. They want one special relationship, and structure the best part of their lives around their homes and families. They need their lives to be settled and organised

Cheerful, gentle and affectionate, they make loyal and loving partners. They will do everything in their power to maintain harmony and make sure their partner is happy. And they give regular hugs and say, "I love you" as part of showing their affection and appreciation of their partner.

Deeply devoted to their children, they are not domineering; in fact they are quite the opposite and if not careful, can be taken advantage of by a demanding and manipulative child.

Dove-Eagles make passionate and creative partners. But they can also be overwhelming in their enthusiasm to 'help' their partner's personal development. Their passion for wanting their partner to 'grow', plus the high expectations they place on them, can become strongly wielded Pygmalion chisels. They do this quite unconsciously and will resent being accused of manipulation, but it is manipulation never the less.

While Dove-Eagles are loving and supportive, they also value independence. If their partner becomes too clingy or over-reliant, they can become quite irritable. If this persists, they may well put their foot down and insist that their partner should stop needing their approval and start making their own decisions.

Thoughtful of others, they rarely, if ever, forget birthdays or anniversaries. And the quickest way to hurt them is to forget theirs.

Dove-Eagles make great companions and mates. They are a continuing source of affection and support to their partners. If you are looking for a loving, compassionate and devoted partner, then you couldn't go past the warm and sensitive Dove-Eagle.

THE DOVE-OWL PARTNER

"It's important to be needed and to help others where you can."

So speaks the Dove-Owl, expressing the guiding philosophy (and the driving need) of all Dove-Owls.

The Dove-Owl is self-consciousness, shy with strangers, speaks quietly and can blush painfully when put in the spotlight. In fact, the last thing they want is to be the centre of attention.

Kind, warm, gentle and timid, they are the people who go out of their way to do almost anything for you. They strive to make themselves indispensable.

They are private people who generally like to keep themselves to themselves. They will rarely initiate a conversation with a stranger, and will only do so if they have to. They are never pushy. At unfamiliar social gatherings, (which can feel quite threatening to them) they will hesitantly stand back from the talking groups, only joining in when they're invited to, rarely giving an opinion, or saying anything that could upset anyone. Being accepted, being tactful, and maintaining harmony — not causing waves —is extremely important to the Dove-Owl.

Bashful, quiet, modest and restrained, they certainly couldn't be labelled as flamboyant or outlandish. They do everything in moderation and avoid anything that may appear over the top, rushed, or in any way risky. It's moderation in all things.

Dove-Owls are loyal and intense to causes and people they care about. They build close relationships with only a small group of trusted friends. To these people, they are trusting, open and generous. To others, they may seem distant.

They like to do things they're comfortable with, things they're familiar with, and they do these in predictable patterns that they rarely alter. Because of this, they tend to find jobs that give them the comfort of repetitive procedures and set structures that offer little risk of sudden change to their normal way of doing things.

In many cases, Dove-Owls are the 'hidden' people who keep the wheels of society turning smoothly for the rest of us. They are the dependable people who work behind the scenes busily doing what has to be done without any noise, fuss or drama.

Dove-Owls generally try to see the good in people and strive to treat others with kindness. But they can also have a critical view of people and can be quick to judge and criticise others harshly. They can also be hard on themselves by being extremely self-critical, castigating themselves for any (human) failings they may have.

Caring, patient and supportive by nature, with great compassion and intuitive skills, they have an almost 'sixth sense' when it comes to what others are feeling. Because of this, they often find careers (more like a 'calling') as social workers, psychologists, counsellors, mentors, nurses, teachers, doctors, volunteers, red cross workers, missionary workers, and the like.

They can often 'bury' themselves in a narrow field of interest, becoming totally absorbed. Some of our most famous poets, romantic novelists, artists and sculptors (today and throughout history) have been Dove-Owls.

The character of the psychiatrist in the movie 'Good Will Hunting', played by Robin Williams, who often plays a Dove-Owl character, is a classic portrayal of the empathetic and caring Dove-Owl doing what they are so naturally good at — counselling, advising, helping and mentoring.

After writing the above, I read a review of the movie 'Bicentennial Man' which also starred Robin Williams. The film critic was unhappy about the film being a vehicle for Robin William's 'niceness'. He felt it was flawed because of his sentimentality and apparent need to be loved by audiences.

The film critic's comment on Robin William's 'need to be loved' sums up the Dove-Owls basic driving force. The need to be loved and to help others is what makes them tick. Robin Williams is a Dove-Owl who usually plays Dove-Owl parts; that's what makes him literally a natural at it.

While on the subject of movies, another one worth seeing for a classic portrayal of a Dove-Owl is 'In The Bedroom'. The husband/father plays the part to a tee, while the wife/mother plays the part of an Eagle-Owl superbly, especially during the scenes after the death of their son.

In a nutshell

Warm, kind and gentle people, Dove-Owls are often referred to as the 'salt of the earth', and I believe they're right. Quiet, unassuming, caring, and totally reliable, they are the people who work behind the scenes. They go about their business every day 'serving the common purpose' in the same way, never making waves, just getting things done. It could also be said that they are the glue that keeps most of our societies and families held together.

Word portrait

Modest, easygoing, pleasant, polite, passive, tranquil, supportive, responsible, dependable, kind, sincere, cooperative, systematic, intuitive, sensitive, considerate, accepting, imaginative, perceptive, adaptable, devoted, sentimental, tender, trusting, compassionate, sympathetic, caring, harmonious, discreet, tactful, diplomatic, solitary, hypersensitive, inhibited, pessimistic, withdrawn, evasive, eccentric, unrealistic, vague.

Wants

They want to maintain harmony.

Admires

They admire people who are trustworthy and loyal.

Influences

They influence others through their modesty, steadiness, and caring attitude.

Strengths

Helpful, dependable, trustworthy, loyal, and patient.

Shortcomings

- Can be too easygoing and accommodating.

- Can be too hesitant in taking the initiative.

- Avoids change.

- Over-avoids risks.

How they communicate

Slower paced and relaxed, Dove-Owls are askers, rather than tellers. They do not force their opinions or values on others. Rather than being assertive, they will advise, recommend, and suggest using questions: "Do you think it would be a good idea if we were to ... ?" "How would you feel if we were to ... ?"

They are also great listeners, especially for whatever ails you. They listen with lots of eye contact and attentive smiles and nods. They show interest through mirroring the facial expressions of those they're conversing with.

Under pressure

Dove-Owls are especially sensitive to disharmony and they will avoid conflict situations at all costs.

Under pressure they tend to become compliant and accommodating. While they may appear to be quietly going along with the other person, deep down inside they are seething. Their defence mechanism is to first silently withdraw, and then quietly fight by becoming stubborn and unmovable.

When their feelings are hurt, (and they can be hurt easily), they withdraw emotionally to both protect themselves, and to punish the other person. Unlike their normal friendly behaviour, when offended, a barrier of ice can suddenly fall which can be a chilling experience for those close to them.

Fears

Change. Unpredictable situations.

Basic Instinct

They are driven by the need to help.

Turn Ons

- To be needed and loved.
- To be indispensable.
- Staying in the background.
- Things to be predictable.
- Sticking to the rules.
- Familiar people and situations.
- Doing one thing at a time.
- Family gatherings.
- Staying home.

Turn Offs

- Not being needed.
- Rejection (of any sort).
- Sudden changes.
- Criticism (of any sort).
- Being put in the spotlight.
- Conflict and disharmony.
- Unfamiliar situations.
- Taking risks.
- Telling people what to do.
- Dealing with difficult people.
- Being forced to do many things at once.
- Parties with strangers.
- Not being able to say "No".
- Being alone.

Common bad feelings

Sense of inadequacy (lack of confidence).

Living with the Dove-Owl

The Dove-Owl is a warm, kind and caring partner. Their need to maintain harmony can create a comfortable, loving and peaceful relationship. Their heart is where their home and family is.

The downside to their quiet and introverted nature is that they tend to keep their feelings to themselves. This could form a wedge in the relationship if the Dove-Owl's partner is an extraverted and expressive personality style. Expressive personality styles want (and need) to talk about feelings — good or bad — the Dove-Owl doesn't.

On the other hand, Dove-Owls can have a critical and judgemental cast of mind and can be quite comfortable telling their loved ones how to behave using 'should' statements and directives. And if their verbal 'shoulds' don't seem to work, they can also exert an influence on their partners with meaningful silences using a strategy of quiet and passive manipulation. While the last thing in the world they want is to dominate their partners, they may be unaware that they are doing it. Rather, they see it as simply helping and caring about their loved ones and will strongly react to the suggestion that it might be pushy, manipulative and playing the Pygmalion Game. But that's certainly what it is.

While Dove-Owls are supportive and caring, they also value independence. If their partner becomes too clingy or over-reliant, they can become quite irritable. If this persists, they may well put their foot down and insist that their partner stop needing their approval and start making their own decisions.

Thoughtful of others, they rarely, if ever, forget birthdays or anniversaries, and the quickest way to hurt them is to forget theirs.

Dove-Owls are a source of continuing love and support to their partners. So, if you are looking for a devoted partner, you couldn't go past the warm and loving Dove-Owl.

THE EXTREME EAGLE PARTNER

"Winning isn't everything — it's the only bloody thing!"

So speaks the Extreme Eagle expressing the guiding philosophy of all Extreme Eagles — win at all cost.

The Extreme Eagle is a confident, no-nonsense, straight-to-the point, totally self-assured person. They are the most controlling, dominant and bossy of all the personality styles — and don't you forget it!

Many people mistakenly assume that being an Eagle is a 'male thing' and being a Dove is a 'female thing'. Nothing could be further from the truth, there are many female Eagles out there as well as many male Doves. Being a Dove, or an Eagle, is not a gender thing. Extreme Eagle men are seen as macho, aggressive, and tough, while unfortunately, women are too often labelled as 'libbers', or 'masculine', or 'not feminine'.

Extreme Eagles are quick talking, quick acting, assertive, and definitely in control of themselves and those around them. They see themselves as strong and want to be the boss in any situation. They believe they were born to tell people what to do. "It's my way — or the highway." They hate not being in control. Even worse, they hate being told what to do.

Extreme Eagles attack life with a sense of urgency. They want everything done yesterday. They live by the expression "Do It Now!" They project a sense of power, energy, and vitality. They move and talk quickly, are forceful and direct and often appear larger than life.

Brave, daring and fearless, their word can be trusted. They work hard to get things done and always finish what they start. Good to have on your side (but not so good to have on the other side!), they are natural fighters who will fight fiercely for what is right and what they believe in.

They also support the underdog and will go to any lengths to protect them. But while they may protect the weak, they despise cowardice and softness. They respect people who stand up for themselves and their ideas, and have no time for those who don't. Pretence is also particularly distasteful to them — they can't stand overly nice or flattering people.

Self-reliant and independent, they are individualists and non-conformists who really don't care what anyone else thinks. Generally unconcerned with style and fashion, their dress is efficient and practical, as are their work surroundings. Their clothes are normally of sober colours, especially dark blues and black.

Achievement and results — getting the job done, is everything to the Extreme Eagle. They absolutely love a challenge. The harder the challenge, the better they like it. That is why to them "Winning isn't everything — it's the only thing!"

Cool, independent and highly competitive, they get short and very impatient with 'lesser mortals'. Intellectual, rather than emotional, they distrust feelings. They are also not too happy about other people expressing their feelings and emotions. That's for wimps.

To the Extreme Eagle, work is a passion. They are the workaholics of life, and will often put work before pleasure (or what some others might call pleasure). To the Extreme Eagle work is not work — it's enjoyment.

When they talk, words are used at a minimum. When asked a question, the Extreme Eagle will give you the short answer — quick and to the point. And unless you ask for more explanation, that's all you're going to get — end of story. Because of this, others can see them as rude and abrupt.

They can be even more bossy and abrupt when those around them are not living up to their high expectations. The quickest way to upset an Extreme Eagle is to give them an excuse, especially a long-winded one, for why you didn't do what you said. If this happens, don't be surprised if you hear them mumble, "God must have loved stupid people, he made so many of them!"

They can be vulnerable and loving with somebody they really care about, and very protective of them. And for all their quick, no-nonsense and assertive approach to people, (which some see as being fierce, intimidating and bullying), they can often surprise those around them with acts of extreme generosity, both with money and acts of kindness that seem to just come out of the blue. Deep down beats a kind heart protected by strong emotional armour.

Extreme Eagles seek respect. Showing them respect for their strength, sharp minds and what they believe are their natural leadership talents is the greatest compliment you can pay them.

In a nutshell

The Extreme Eagle is a confident, fast, competitive person who gets things done — quickly — and with a minimum of fuss. They are the Doers of the world. History is full of them as Generals and the like. (As mentioned before, being an Eagle is not a male thing; there are also plenty of female Eagles in the history books). No matter where they are they will want to be in charge. They are the controllers. They like to be the boss. They are goal-oriented workaholics who normally get what they set out for. They are impatient with slower-moving people, and they can have a low tolerance for the feelings and advice of others. Achievement and results are everything. They love a challenge and the freedom to achieve their objective their way. One of their biggest turn-offs is being bored and unchallenged.

Word portrait

Confident, controlling, fast, businesslike, cool, no-nonsense, competitive, independent, assertive, self-disciplined, positive, self-reliant, productive, bold, bossy, rational, decisive, forceful, quick, impatient, blunt, critical, undiplomatic, driven, frank, leader, logical, intolerant, resolute, focused, efficient, systematic, responsible, rigid, doer, pragmatic, enthusiastic, objective, succinct, planner, competent, workaholic, unbending, tough, determined, ambitious, domineering, strong-willed, aggressive.

Wants

Achievement. Results. Challenge. To be the boss.

Admires

People who take responsibility and can get things done fast.

Influences

They influence others through their ability to independently get what they set out for.

Strengths

Making decisions. Getting results. Causing action.

Shortcomings

- Not comfortable at being 'one of the mob', wants to always be the boss.

- Not good at using caution.

- Can go to extreme lengths to achieve their goals.

- Can be disruptive when bored.

- Can be bullying, intimidating and rude, especially to Dove personality types.

- Can be totally oblivious to the feelings and little 'people things' that are happening around them.

How they communicate

Straight-faced and rather humourless, their body language is fast and efficient. Facial expressions are generally unemotional and controlled. Little animation is shown when they speak.

They are direct and honest, they put their cards on the table. They speak their mind and shoot straight from the hip. You know exactly where they stand.

They have little patience for small talk. They like to keep their conversations brief, and to the point — and they like to stick to the facts. They get extremely uncomfortable talking about feelings, or 'touchy-feely' issues. In fact they will avoid these types of conversations like the plague.

Always preoccupied with their own thoughts, they are hopeless listeners, unless of course, the conversation interests them — and not many do.

They often describe (rationalise) their bluntness as simply being 'frank and honest' when in reality others see it as blunt and rude.

Because they like excitement and stimulation, they will often create conflict and verbally spar with people. If things get heated they can be street fighters — they don't pull their punches — and they can punch below the belt.

Under pressure

If things aren't going their way, the Extreme Eagle becomes domineering and bossy and can be a bully. They assert themselves more than normal (which is saying something!) but rather than being loud, they do it in a cool (cold) unemotional way using facts and words like weapons.

Under stress, they can become venomously sarcastic. And if things don't get better, the Extreme Eagle will turn off by avoiding, or ignoring, (or both) the person causing the stress. The Extreme Eagle fights, then flights.

They have a hard time admitting their mistakes (a mistake would be a weakness) and they don't say sorry too often.

Fears

Nearness. (Don't get too close). Also fears not being in control.

Basic Instinct

They are driven by the need to be in control — and get results.

Turn Ons

- Winning.
- Challenge.
- Work.
- Getting results.
- Leading and controlling others.
- Being shown respect.
- People who stand up for themselves.

Turn Offs

- Losing.
- Boredom — not being challenged.
- Emotional displays.
- Not being in control.
- Being told what to do.
- Long-winded excuses.

- Cowardice or softness.
- Being patient.
- Waiting (for anything).
- Slow-moving people.
- Listening.

Common bad feelings

Worry — that they are not achieving what they should be.

Living with the Extreme Eagle

As in any relationship, a relationship with an Extreme Eagle takes understanding. When you understand the Extreme Eagle's need to be in charge, and understand that they are fiercely protective of those they love, and if you are willing to accept the controlling aspects of their personality, then their protective nature can be very comforting.

When the chips are down, and everything around you is falling to pieces, you couldn't have a stronger pillar of strength to take charge (and lean on) than an Extreme Eagle. Just don't expect that they're going to get all lovey-dovey after they've cleaned up the mess. They won't.

Also, you will need to accept the fact that they may well put their careers before their relationships. To live in harmony this must be accepted, because challenge and work is the Extreme Eagle's oxygen. Without it they cannot survive. So, expect to spend some time alone.

Time away from work, like holidays, or what most of us would call relaxation, is hard work for them. In a word, boring. Generally their holiday activities look more like hard work to the rest of us. So, when it comes to having a holiday with an Extreme Eagle, be prepared for some abseiling, rough water rafting — or climbing a mountain!

Don't expect too many loving cuddles, and all that other lovey-dovey stuff. It's not going to happen. They are not big on giving praise either. They don't need it, and can't see why you should.

As a parent, the Extreme Eagle is protective, (sometimes overprotective), caring, and devoted. On the other hand, they can be demanding, controlling, and rigid.

In a relationship Extreme Eagles can be very protective, loyal, caring, positive, truthful, straightforward, committed, generous and supportive. On the downside they can be demanding, arrogant, combative, possessive, uncompromising, and quick to find fault.

Be prepared for the quick decisions they will make, especially the ones you feel you should have been consulted on, but wasn't. It's going to happen.

If you are prepared to be confident, stand up for yourself, be direct, don't betray their trust, give them space to be alone and don't assume their direct approach is a personal attack, then the Extreme Eagle just might be the partner for you.

THE EAGLE-PEACOCK PARTNER

"The only place success comes before work is in the dictionary."

So states an Eagle-Peacock expressing a guiding principle that all Eagle-Peacocks live by.

Their self-image is linked to achieving and winning. They are the most ambitious of all the personality styles. They are the 'Achievers'.

The hardest work an Eagle-Peacock can do is to be idle. They tend to put work before other things and never run out of things to do. They are always busy. Illness rarely stops them. Their hyperactive imagination is always occupied with new projects. Fast-thinking and quick acting, they are always on the move. They go flat out until the job is done and get it done in the shortest possible time. Energetic, goal directed and totally focused, they can do more in a day than most people can in a week.

Intelligent, self-disciplined, dynamic and productive, they are good at many things. Confident, friendly and outgoing, they approach life with optimism and enthusiasm. They generally feel pretty good about themselves and see themselves as winners even before they are.

They make what they do look easy, but they work hard for their success and people naturally (and quite wrongly) assume they don't need to be praised. But everything they do is for praise. They cannot be praised enough. And if it is not forthcoming, they'll send out subtle messages in order to rake it in.

Cheerful people with a sunny disposition, they are charming and have a way of making people feel special and important. They radiate confidence, have a natural ease and assurance, and have the ability to inspire others to go along with them. Socially poised and self-assured, they are comfortable in almost any social situation. In fact, they rather like socialising, especially if it means being recognised in public.

Good-humoured, they laugh easily and are witty and stimulating company. Persuasive communicators, they are both skilful in using language, and emotional and logical reasons, to sway others to their way of thinking. Depending on the situation, (and who they are talking to), they can be either charming or intimidating.

Achievement is everything to the Eagle-Peacock. They are always looking for new challenges. Yesterday's achievements are just that —

yesterday's. They never rest on past glories, or savour their successes for too long. And they are never satisfied. Their next achievement must always be bigger and better than the last. People often look to them to run the show.

They are individualists who hate to be seen as 'soft', and fear being manipulated (and especially conned) in any way, yet at the same time they can be quite capable of manipulating others.

Goal-setters and doers, they will work tirelessly until the goal is achieved. They can't leave a job unfinished; it plays on their mind. It must be done — and done now. They hate half finished jobs, and until it is done, they will block out all other thoughts and distractions, becoming so absorbed in the task that they lose all sense of time. They love nature, and find in it one of the few places they can truly relax and be at peace.

Eagle-Peacocks are result-getters. While others are thinking about how and when to do it, the Eagle-Peacock has done it. Problem Solvers Extraordinaire, they love being challenged. Telling them, "It can't be done" is one of the quickest ways to motivate them into action. Given time, they will do everything in their power to prove that it can be done. Efficient, inventive, and non-conformist by nature, they hate to hear, "This is the way it's done, because we've always done it this way." If there is a faster, cheaper, or more efficient way of doing it, the Eagle-Peacock will find it — or invent it.

They have a hunger for knowledge and know-how, but unlike Owl-type personalities who like to learn simply for the sake of learning, the Eagle-Peacock learns in order to use the knowledge to advance their career.

They make excellent leaders. Good at 'handling' people, they have an intuitive feel for people-politics and a keen interest in human nature. They know what makes people tick and are experts at creating team spirit and motivating them to get the job done.

They make popular leaders, but they also value their independence. They are more than happy to do their 'own thing' without the need for a team around them. (They find it hard to stand still and wait patiently for the stragglers.) In fact, they prefer to work alone accepting the applause when they win or taking the blame if they fail — which isn't often. But if they do fail, they bounce back quickly.

Generous, (sometimes to a fault), when they have abundance, they want the people they care about to share it with them. It has been said they will give you the shirt off their backs.

Adventurous risk-takers and entrepreneurs at heart, they enjoy working independently without anyone looking over their shoulder (which they detest), and they are effective operators of their own businesses. But because they detest routine work, they need help in doing their bookwork (which they hate) and guidance when it comes to spending money, which they love!

Born actors, they are always conscious of how they present themselves. They like to stand out from the crowd. They dress and talk to impress, and like chameleons, they can instantly change to suit the occasion — both in how they look and what they say. They are excellent at selling themselves and their ideas, especially as public speakers. Many of our so-called 'motivational speakers' are Eagle-Peacocks. They can really move a crowd. And they love the applause that follows.

They can stretch the truth in order to make something, or themselves, look good. They are not bald-faced liars as such, but they can certainly 'embellish the truth' to make it sound better. The broken promises of politicians (many of whom are Eagle-Peacocks) are classic examples of this 'embellishment syndrome'.

In the movies they are often portrayed as a combination of naked ambition coupled with savvy street smarts. The character of 'Gekko', the stock market wheeler-dealer, played by Michael Douglas in the movie "Wall Street" is a classic portrayal of the Eagle-Peacock in full flight. Risk-taking, impulsive decision-making, entrepreneurial skills, and the pursuit of wealth and recognition are all part of the Eagle-Peacock's make up.

In a nutshell

The Eagle-Peacock is cheerful, socially confident, warm, charming and witty. Enthusiastic, optimistic and adventurous risk-takers, they are result-orientated goal-setters who work with creative and sustained energy to achieve recognition, prestige and wealth. They hate being locked into 'ordinary jobs' or monotonous routines. They are imaginative and competitive with good verbal skills and are invariably popular.

Word portrait

Confident, outgoing, talkative, cheerful, friendly, charming, sociable, outspoken, popular, enthusiastic, energetic, humorous, animated, motivating, optimistic, intellectual, persuasive, unselfconscious, structured, punctual, organised, intuitive, imaginative, inventive, insightful, lucid, logical, rational, objective, succinct, adaptable, easygoing, flexible, adventurous, mobile, daring, argumentative, impatient, intolerant, over-forceful.

Wants

To be rich and famous.

Admires

Achievers and adventurers — those who have 'made it'.

Influences

They influence others through their charm and self-motivation, and their ability to get things done — fast.

Strengths

Ambition, energy, vision.

Shortcomings

- Can compare themselves to others too much and become jealous of other's success.

- Can become impatient and over-forceful when things aren't going their way.

- Can over-spend to 'look good'.

- Can have moods of high highs and very low lows.

- Can have angry periods.

How they communicate

Mentally agile, alert, witty and outspoken, Eagle-Peacocks pride themselves on both their ability to communicate and skill in using language. They are good with words and can use them just as easily to persuade as to attack. They have little time for people who are vague or use language poorly.

With their curious minds and an interest in just about everything, they can be fascinating conversationalists. But they are terrible listeners, especially when it comes to small talk, which they find impossible to handle and a waste of time and effort. Also, too often in a relationship, they don't give their partner their full attention when he/she talks, but expect it when they talk.

They are also terrible listeners when it comes to 'just wanting to talk' about a problem. Rather than 'just' listening with a sympathetic ear, they'll jump in with advice.

During a conversation, because they enjoy a 'verbal joust', (and are serious one-upmanship game players), they may abruptly change their opinion and deliberately debate and argue for an opposite view, just for the fun of it. Depending on whom they are conversing with, this can either be mentally stimulating or just downright tiring.

Under pressure

Eagle-Peacocks like to be organised and in control of things, or they worry and fuss and become cranky which can be straining times for their partners. When they get anxious, (or to avoid emotional pressure), they jump into activity and totally immerse themselves in their projects.

Under pressure, their sharp mind can be backed-up with an equally sharp tongue. The upside is that once they've got it out, it's quickly over. They don't brood on past slights or hold grudges. "Let's move on" is a guiding principle of the Eagle-Peacock.

Fears

Being 'ordinary'.

Basic Instinct

They are driven by the need for public recognition of their accomplishments.

Turn Ons

- Prestige and financial security through achievement.
- Public recognition and applause.
- Taking risks.
- Challenging work.
- Getting the job done — quickly.
- Persuading others.
- Nature.
- Knowledge.
- Independence.
- Spending money.

Turn Offs

- Failure — being ordinary — not being seen as successful.
- Not receiving recognition for accomplishments.
- Boredom.
- Criticism.
- Being manipulated.
- Half-finished jobs.
- Rules and regulations.
- Being told what to do.
- Routine work.
- Paperwork.
- Having to read the instruction manual.

Common bad feelings

Worry and anger.

Living with the Eagle-Peacock

Eagle-Peacocks are generally easygoing, 'live-and-let-live' people who seek to maintain harmony in their relationships.

Financial security is important to them. They work hard to take care and provide for their family and will do all in their power to create a comfortable and well-presented home for their partner and children, (as well as to look good to the outside world), and they will often go into debt to do it.

Self-disciplined in their work habits, they can seem almost careless when it comes to spending on their homes, cars, furniture, holidays and other creature comforts. Eagle-Peacocks believe they need a higher income than 'normal people' in order to maintain the type of lifestyle they believe they deserve. As a result, they need a partner who is 'more grounded' and who is certainly better at handling the domestic finances.

When the Eagle-Peacock is up, they're really up. But when they're down, they're down, which can make it difficult for a partner to know just what to do.

Family is important to them. The Eagle-Peacock constantly struggles between wanting to spend time with their kids and wanting to get more work done. As a result, they can be inconsistent with the attention they give their children. They can be warm and affectionate when with them, but can neglect them when they're absorbed in their work or outside interests. If possible, they will happily leave the day-to-day rearing of the children to their partner.

As a parent, they are generally easygoing, consistent, dependable and loyal, and in return they expect their children to be responsible and organised. They value independence and believe that people grow through experience and overcoming challenges. Eagle-Peacocks encourage their children to spread their wings and 'have a go', and as a result, they usually gain their independence quickly and fly on their own wings earlier than most.

Because they live by the principle of 'live and let live', they are not usually big Pygmalion Game players and rarely nag. But they can become impatient and start chiselling on a partner who takes an emotional, rather than a logical, view of things.

Romantic, loving, and sentimental, birthdays and anniversaries are celebrated with gifts and dinners out, along with the occasional dirty weekend (and perhaps a self-written love poem) to keep the romance alive.

They usually have many acquaintances but just a few close friends, to whom they are true friends — helpful, caring and reliable. To their loved ones, they are fiercely protective, loving and loyal. But because they can become so absorbed in achieving their goals (working towards becoming rich and famous), there may be times when their partner may well get the feeling of playing a poor second fiddle. But if you understand and can accept that this is what drives them — what makes them tick — then one thing is for sure; life won't be boring living with the Eagle-Peacock.

THE EAGLE-DOVE PARTNER

"I did it my way."

So sang the late Frank Sinatra, singing the theme song of all Eagle-Doves.

Eagle-Doves are sometimes hard to spot. They are calm, easygoing, seem a bit on the shy side, and can be hard to get to know.

While friendly, they can seem socially withdrawn. They are not comfortable with small talk or idle chitchat. They prefer their own company. Rather than socialising and talking trivialities, they would much rather be reading, or working on a challenging problem, or just plain doing something more constructive.

They are, loyal, friendly and tactful people who have a very clearly defined set of goals and an unbending set of personal values, coupled with a deep sense of duty towards the people and organisations they care about, and will refuse to stay in situations where their values are compromised or their goals frustrated.

They are initiators with a sense of mission — they make things happen.

They hate being locked into a routine, or forced to do repetitive work. They like to take creative and inventive ideas and put them to use. Energetic and conscientious, they are good with technology and enjoy designing systems, models and structures that help to bring about organisation and order.

They are rarely idle or at loose ends looking for something to do. Achievement-orientated, they are always looking for new challenges to conquer. Yesterday's achievements are just that — yesterday's. Eagle-Doves never rest on their laurels, or savour their successes for too long. And they are never satisfied. Their next achievement must always be bigger and better than the last.

They concentrate deeply on the task at hand, and can work on it tirelessly to the point where they lose all sense of time, even between night and day. But once having completed it, they will quickly put it behind them and move on to other ideas and challenges.

They have a high opinion of their personal ability and can happily play the role of either leader, or follower — and are good at both. But they would prefer to work alone, quietly and diligently — and without interruption. They are individualists. Win or lose, they're prepared to take either the applause or the blame. The song, 'I Did It My Way' was written for the Eagle-Dove.

Eagle-Doves can be hard taskmasters, both on themselves, and if leaders, on those in the team. They want results and expect to get them. But they also have the knack of remaining popular with the 'troops' even though they find it hard to delegate important tasks. They worry it won't be done properly.

Generally calm and unflappable, they don't get too excited about anything, and tend not to worry about things that are beyond their control.

They rarely join groups, and are not often found at meetings; if they do, they won't stay long.

Their word can be trusted. Coupled with their strong resolve and dogged willpower, if they say they'll do something, or *not* do something, then you can bet that's exactly what will happen. You know exactly where you stand with an Eagle-Dove.

In a nutshell

Eagle-Doves are private individualists. They are energetic, inventive and loyal people who have a deep sense of duty towards the people and organisations they care about. Conscientious and diligent, they have a high opinion of their personal worth, and strong commitments to personal and traditional values. Initiators and achievers with a definite sense of mission and direction, they immerse themselves 'boots and all' in jobs and interests that challenge them.

Word portrait

Quiet, reserved, friendly, private, ethical, individualist, deep, optimistic, independent, resolute, doer, energetic, initiator, dependable, intuitive, imaginative, pragmatic, inventive, creative, logical, objective, succinct, analytical, adaptable, conscientious, loyal, versatile, diligent, competent, self-reliant, strong-willed, inflexible, perfectionist, businesslike, unsociable, aloof, inhibited, withdrawn, unrealistic, impatient, argumentative, intolerant.

Wants

To work independently to achieve personal goals.

Admires

People who have achieved success through intelligence and integrity.

Influences

They influence others with their initiative and ability to act alone to get results.

Strengths

High personal standards.

Shortcomings

- Overuses self-reliance.

- Can be too much of a loner.

- Can be fussy.

How they communicate

Eagle-Doves have little time for small talk and less time for 'nonsense' when it comes to conversing.

Mentally agile and alert, Eagle-Doves pride themselves on both their thinking ability, and their skill in using language precisely — and they expect others to be just as precise.

Even in a casual conversation, they'll pick up on anything that sounds inconsistent, or doesn't ring true. When they hear it, they'll pounce on it immediately, point it out and correct it. This can come across to some as arrogant and often make a conversation with them both uncomfortable and plain hard work.

They pride themselves on their ingenuity, have a good memory, and are confident in their knowledge of what they're about. This can sometimes result in them being impatient with 'lesser mortals' who are not 'up with it' and can also make them appear a bit snobbish.

They enjoy a 'verbal joust' and can be ruthless debaters. Therefore, it pays those who are not as verbally sharp as the Eagle-Dove, to keep right away from any type of adversarial discussion with them.

Under pressure

Generally calm and unflappable, under pressure they can become even cooler than normal. Or they can become short, impatient, blunt and critical. They can often be heard saying, "If you want a job done properly, then do it yourself."

Fears

Others involved with them may have lesser personal standards.

Basic Instinct

They are driven by the need to do things their way.

Turn Ons

- Achievement.
- Independence.
- Knowledge.
- Challenging work.
- Doing one's duty.
- Taking the initiative.
- Putting ideas into practical use.

Turn Offs

- Not being challenged.
- Not getting results.
- Being idle.
- Boredom.
- Routine work.
- Meetings.
- Parties.

Common bad feelings

Worry and inadequacy.

Living with the Eagle-Dove

As partners, Eagle-Doves are faithful and devoted and take the relationship very seriously. They strive for harmony, are kind, even-tempered and easy to live with.

They have a definite sense of the right way and the wrong way of doing things. They like to maintain a sense of order in the home by following established and predictable patterns.

Almost always preoccupied with their thoughts, they can be forgetful of appointments, birthdays, anniversaries and family ceremonies.

Not being a 'social creature', they prefer their own company, and that of their family. They are not happy about having parties and social activities at home — and will never initiate or organise them. When it comes to organising social outings and the like, they will leave it up to their partner.

Eagle-Doves enjoy children and are devoted parents. They are serious about their children's upbringing, treating each child as an individual with rights, privileges and as much freedom (which they themselves value highly) as they can handle. They rarely, if ever, attack their children physically or verbally.

They generally keep their feelings to themselves and can appear rather insensitive to a more emotional partner.

If you're prepared to meet their high standards, and don't mind not having too many parties, then the Eagle-Dove may well be the partner for you.

THE EAGLE-OWL PARTNER

"You're doing that wrong. Here, let me show you how to do it my way — the right way."

Eagle-Owls spend a lot of their time telling people how to do things. Often called 'The Perfectionists', they seem to go through life as 'Guardians of the Right Way' believing that the world is not a safe and orderly place unless he or she is watching everyone's behaviour and attitude, and making corrections. They make sure things are done carefully and with perfection.

They give the impression of being cool, aloof and hard to get to know — standoffish. Socialising and small talk is not one of their preferred activities. Although they can be quite charming when they want to be.

Eagle-Owls are rational people. They trust and use logic to make sense of things. As far as they are concerned, emotions and feelings are not to be trusted and play little part in the scheme of things. They never let their heart rule their head.

They absolutely hate being locked into a routine, and they detest doing repetitive work. They have original and inventive minds. They seek out unusual and creative challenges, are excellent problem solvers, and posses a high drive factor for achievement.

They were the bright kids at school who studied and read far beyond what was being taught, and could answer any question put to them by the teacher, but wouldn't unless they were directly asked. They didn't have to. They knew they were bright and had no need to prove it to anyone. They kept themselves to themselves — and still do.

With their self-assured confidence plus their economy with words added to their cool 'unemotional' approach, they can often give the impression of being arrogant.

Highly efficient, they value time and don't waste it, especially on small talk, or on people who offer little in the way of intellectual stimulation, and even less on those who have nothing to 'offer.'

Goal-orientated, they want to get results in the shortest possible time. Driven by the need to achieve, and result-orientated, they are invariably chronic workaholics and over-achievers.

Achievement is the thing. They are always looking for new challenges. Yesterday's achievements are just that — yesterday's. Eagle-Owls never rest on past glories, or savour their successes for too long. They are never satisfied and their next achievement must always be bigger and better than the last.

Doing better also flows over to their sporting and recreational pursuits. Grim-faced and intent on winning, when one watches them at 'play', it can seem like work. Urged on by the killer instinct, it's never 'just a game' to the Eagle-Owl.

Take-charge people with a commanding nature, many of our military leaders and politicians (both male and female) throughout history have been Eagle-Owls. Task-orientated, rather than people-orientated, being liked and popular is not important to them. But respect is. They would rather be respected for their accomplishments, than for winning a popularity contest, any day.

Also called 'The Controller' or 'The Boss' personality, they have definite and unbending opinions of how things should be done. Some who work with them, say there are only two ways to do something — their way and the wrong way. Their "I-am-right-and-you-are-wrong" approach often loses them potential supporters they could have had if only they would yield the less important points in order to win the most important. So often they win the battle, but lose the war, when it comes to the 'people side' of things.

Their word can be trusted. Coupled with their strong resolve and dogged willpower, if they say they'll do something, or *not* do something, then you can bet that's exactly what will happen. You know exactly where you stand with an Eagle-Owl.

Analytic and perfectionists, they will split hairs and nitpick. Born sceptics, everything must be proven — using only logic and reason. Any appeal with a hint of 'emotional reasoning' will be discarded by them immediately, and under their breath they may well say, "God must have loved stupid people, he made so many of them!"

The character of Harry Callaghan played by Clint Eastwood in the movie; 'Dirty Harry' is a classic portrayal of the Eagle-Owl — strong, cool, unemotional and tight-lipped.

While on the subject of movies, another one worth seeing for a classic portrayal of an Eagle-Owl is 'In The Bedroom'. The wife/mother plays the part to a tee, while the husband/father plays the part of a Dove-Owl superbly, especially during the scenes after the death of their son.

In a nutshell

The Eagle-Owl is confident, independent, decisive and determined. Trivialities, socialising and small talk does not interest them. Yet there are times when they can be quite outgoing and charming. Systematic and objective, they are interested in the unusual and creative. They have a natural ability to plan, organise and get things done — with or without help. They strive to get results with accuracy bordering on perfectionism. Sceptical and stubborn, they have definite and unbending opinions of right and wrong in both their personal and professional lives and expect others to comply with them.

Word portrait

Independent, formal, solitary, reserved, responsible, intellectual, inventive, rational, logical, objective, realistic, effective, organised, determined, efficient, rigorous, accurate, exacting, perfectionist, pragmatic, intuitive, imaginative, ingenious, insightful, lucid, planner, succinct, aloof, cool, blunt, withdrawn, rigid, impatient, argumentative, arrogant, intolerant, sceptical, critical, stubborn.

Wants

Mental and intellectual stimulation. Unusual and creative challenges.

Admires

Inventive achievers, and those with high personal standards.

Influences

They influence others through their no-nonsense approach to solving problems and overcoming challenges.

Strengths

Self-motivated, disciplined, calculated risk-taker, planner, organiser, change-maker, result-getter.

Shortcomings

- Perfectionism.

- Hardnosed — puts tasks before people.

- Can over-use criticism and bluntness.

- Lacks tolerance for the everyday foibles of human nature.

How they communicate

Eagle-Owls are tellers (commanders), not askers. They communicate in a lecturing, teaching style.

Eagle-Owls can appear to be (and usually are) preoccupied with their own thoughts rather than intent on listening.

When speaking, they can be blunt and to the point. They have no time, or desire for trivialities, or to employ the 'social niceties,' which can often come across as rude and uncaring. On the other hand, when you ask them a question, you will invariably get the 'long answer' — they have an opinion on almost everything — and you will get it, chapter and verse.

Under pressure

They don't get too enthusiastic or excited about anything that's beyond their control. But they do worry and fuss over the things that are in their control.

Normally calm and unflappable, under pressure they become even cooler than normal.

When things aren't going their way they can become critical and bossy using 'cool logic' as their weapon of choice. And if things don't get any better, they can become sulky and withdrawn, and deliberately avoid the person or situation which is causing them problems.

Possessing a strong sense of justice, if they feel they have been conned, or taken advantage of in any way, they will boil with a sense of injustice — and for a long time. Getting revenge, no matter how long it may take, can be very sweet to the Eagle-Owl.

Fears

Not being in control and being bored and unchallenged.

Basic Instinct

They are driven by the need for achievement and 'correct' results.

Turn Ons

- Work.
- Challenge.
- Achievement.
- Winning.
- Independence.
- Being in control.
- Correctness (Perfection).
- People who take a logical approach.
- Being respected (rather than popular).

Turn Offs

- Losing.
- Not being challenged.
- Routine work.
- Not being in control.
- Irrational approaches and displays of emotion.
- People who do things 'wrong'.
- People who waste their time with excuses.
- Wishy washy people.

Common bad feelings

Suppressed anger and an impending sense of failure.

Living with the Eagle-Owl

Fierce protectors and good providers, the Eagle-Owls show their love and affection by providing a secure and stable environment for their partners and offspring.

Away from the hurly burly of the outside world, they seek peace, harmony and order in their home and relationship.

As they are generally loners who like their privacy, they usually only have a few close friends.

Entertaining at home 'just for the fun of it' is really no fun for the Eagle-Owl.

With their perfectionist bent, and their, "I'm right and you are wrong" attitude, plus their controlling nature, they can be quite demanding and difficult to satisfy. With their definite views of right and wrong, they can be deft Pygmalion chisellers.

More emotional partners claim they can be insensitive, distant and cool, or even seem uncaring when it comes to the emotional side of things. But this is generally not true, for deep inside they are quite passionate about their loved ones. They're just not 'into' sharing their feelings. Controlled at all times, they keep a tight rein on their emotions and impulses. They are especially 'turned off' by public displays of emotion.

Don't expect too many words of endearment and "I love you's." An Eagle-Owl's commitment to the relationship is total. "I love you" goes without saying. As far as the Eagle-Owl is concerned, there's no need to state the bleeding obvious!

The reason they can give the impression of being distant and aloof, or not quite with you, is that they're invariably deep in thought. They get caught up and preoccupied with thinking about things — ideas, problems, work and the like, or they'll be reading (always non-fiction), or studying in their never ending pursuit of knowledge and 'How To'. Added to all this is their ability to be able to 'lock in,' to totally focus and concentrate on one thing at a time, completely shutting out any other thoughts and interruptions — and people.

For better, or for worse, this makes them quite oblivious to all the 'little people things' that's going on around them. It can also make their partners feel excluded and 'shut out' from their world. Yet while they may be unaware of what's happening around them, when this apparent 'distance' is pointed out to them, they can become quite concerned and responsive. So, every now and again it pays to remind them to change their mental focus and join the family circle — mentally as well physically.

Many a relationship with an Eagle-Owl has hit the rocks because a 'more emotional' partner has not wanted to ask ("Why should I have to ask?") for more attention, expecting it to 'just happen.' They wait angrily for it to happen, and fume when it doesn't. It won't just happen out of the blue — Eagle-Owls need to be reminded. And when they are, they can be as loving and as caring as the rest of us.

The Eagle-Owl values independence highly. They would die for it. If they feel the slightest hint that their independence and freedom is being restricted, they will resent it and resist it.

Wanting their own independence, they want their mate to be too. The last thing they want is for their partner to be dependant on them for their interests and happiness — to live through them. Their partner should have a life of his or her own, with his or her own interests.

They hate being told what to do. If a request even slightly sounds like a command, or an order, they'll dig their heels in. Nobody tells an Eagle-Owl what to do. But having said that, if asked 'properly,' Eagle-Owls will do just about anything for their partner.

Because they prize 'strength of character,' and abhor weakness, they admire those who can stand up for themselves (especially against them) and disrespect those who can't. As a result, they want a partner who values their independence as much as they do, and who is certainly not overly submissive.

They believe that children develop and grow through having their independence and meeting life's challenges head-on. As a result, Eagle-Owls encourage it in their children, but within well-defined limits and rules which they clearly set. Because of this, the children of Eagle-Owls usually fly on their own wings earlier than most.

Once having set the rules, because they are prone to be workaholics, Eagle-Owls can tend to neglect their children because they become so absorbed in their own work. If possible they will happily leave the day-to-day rearing of the children to their partner.

So, don't expect too much lovey-dovey stuff, and be prepared to sometimes take second place to the 'achievement factor.' But if you are looking for a partner who will bring unfailing protection and stability to a relationship, then the Eagle-Owl may be the partner for you.

THE EXTREME OWL PARTNER

"Fools rush in where wise men fear to tread. Don't take chances. Play it safe. You can't get your fingers burnt that way."

So speaks the Extreme Owl on behalf of all Extreme Owls. 'Playing it safe' — in everything — is their guiding philosophy of life. And they stick to it religiously.

Careful to a fault and deep thinkers, Extreme Owls are our solid citizens. They take life very seriously. Thoughtful and introspective, they appear shy, cool and distant. Quiet, analytical, reserved and poker-faced, they show little, if any, outward feelings or emotions and can be very hard to get to know. They view life with detached objectivity — they are observers, not players. They are the most retiring and introverted of all the personality styles.

Conservative, tender, gentle, and polite, they tend to wear neutral and sober colours, especially brown and fawn tones. They often wear glasses and have done from an early age. They have little preoccupation with clothes, fashion or style — little sense of 'what goes with what' — nor do they care.

They rely on habitual structure, orderliness, and systems — things they are familiar with to guide them through an uncertain world. In the Extreme Owl's world there is a place for everything and everything is in its place.

They are always on guard. The world can be a scary place for the Extreme Owl. Cautious and extremely conservative, they are definitely not risk takers. Nor are they socialisers. Independent and individualistic, they prefer and enjoy their own company — they like their privacy and solitude. They can spend hours reading, gardening, playing music, or involvement in some 'intellectual' hobby.

Extreme Owls are thinkers, rather than feelers. They deal in facts, not emotions. They are always looking for the logic in something.

Because human beings are not logical creatures, the 'reasoning' behind the emotional (illogical) behaviour of others, leaves the Extreme Owl completely baffled. That's why they prefer to deal with things (numbers, formulas, machinery etc) that are logical and predictable, rather than with people, who are not.

Prone to being suspicious and sceptical, (they see the glass half empty, not half full) they're always looking for 'the catch'. They want to see the proof, the evidence, the facts. They want ironclad guarantees, especially when buying something. They can take forever to make a decision and tend to buy only the tried and proven, which to them is the most low risk 'logical' and 'safest' decision to make. They will often use the saying, "Fools rush in where wise men fear to tread", to justify taking so long to make a decision, or to take action.

Intensely analytical, they find safety in knowledge and can't seem to get enough of it. They will study a subject just for the sake of learning about it, rather than to use the information. They are systematic, structured and thorough. They want order in all things and focus only on one thing at a time and will resist being sidetracked.

They don't like to have things thrown at them suddenly. When it comes to getting a decision, or some action, from an Extreme Owl, they need warning and plenty of time to think and plan ahead. They need to cover all the bases. That's why they're always writing 'Things To Do' lists. They need things to be on paper. The spoken word doesn't count.

Extreme Owls have a strong belief in traditional authority, and great respect for rules and accepted procedures, law and order. And they obey them to the letter — and expect everyone else to.

In a nutshell

The Extreme Owl is a quiet, serious, practical, and reserved person who is cautious and conservative in almost everything they do. They can appear distant and aloof to some. They take a no-nonsense approach to almost everything they do. They are dependable, trustworthy, and reliable partners who like to follow set routines and patterns. They are logical and systematic and like to 'go by the book' irrespective of whether it's the Rule Book, the Bible, or the Procedure Manual.

Word portrait

Withdrawn, conservative, quiet, stable, serious, formal, detached, curious, thinker, respectable, reserved, predictable, loner, deep, organised, logical, objective, systematic, thorough, practical, orderly, matter of fact, responsible, efficient, succinct, discreet, aloof, inhibited, withdrawn, precise, reliable, detailed, dull, fussy, impatient, rigid, obsessive, intolerant, argumentative, pessimistic, realistic, dependable, steadfast, trustworthy, determined, perfectionist, unsociable, indecisive.

Wants

Security through set procedures, facts, data, law and order. No risk. No change.

Admires

Conservatism and correctness.

Influences

They influence others through being dependable, accurate and precise.

Strengths

Diligent, organised, precise, systematic, persistent, and trustworthy.

Shortcomings

♦ Pessimistic

♦ Over relies on rules, habits and procedures.

♦ Can be stiff, picky and righteous.

♦ Slow at making decisions.

How they communicate

Their voice is soft, calm and soothing — they never shout. Their body language displays little, if any, animation or spontaneity. They use very little emotion, or facial expressions, when communicating. Often referred to as 'poker faced'. They have a dry sense of humour.

When they communicate they deal in facts, not feelings. They will avoid emotional issues.

They are good listeners, because they pay close attention to detail.

When you ask them a question, the Extreme Owl (as with all Owl types) will give you 'the long answer', whether you wanted it or not.

They quote numbers, figures and statistics — and they're always accurate.

They seem to know everything about everything, and will go into infinite detail to tell you about it, whether you want to hear it or not. It has been said that when you ask an Owl the time, they will tell you how a clock works!

Extreme Owls (as do all Owls) spend a lot of time internally debating all the options before coming to a decision. They need to be given this time to feel comfortable. So, before you ask them, "What do you think we should do?" give them plenty of time to think about it — don't rush them.

Under pressure

They think before they act. They 'feel' through their head. It is important to them to maintain calm. No one can tell by their looks how they're feeling inside, whether it's a red-hot rage or blissful happiness. This can make them seem snooty and cold, but in reality they have as intense emotions as the rest of us, it's just that they are delayed.

They can creep inside themselves when danger approaches. If forced to make a quick decision, the Owl will avoid. They will put things off till later — perhaps for forever! When put under too much pressure, the Extreme Owl becomes worried and fussy.

When put under the stress of having to do something they don't agree with, or don't want to do, they will do a slow burn and play the 'mute withdrawal game'. They will retreat into silence. This is the game of 'quiet and passive manipulation'. This 'silence and solitude treatment' works well for them because it causes confrontation without them seeming to initiate it.

Fears

Unpredictability. The unexpected. Acting without hard facts, or a proven system.

Basic Instinct

They are driven by the need for certainty — the need to be right.

Turn Ons

- Certainty and predictability.
- Correctness.
- Proven facts.
- Systems, patterns and habits.
- Knowledge and information.
- Solitude and privacy.
- Gardening and nature.
- Law and order, rules and regulations.
- The tried and the proven.
- Being respected.

Turn Offs

- Not being right.
- Taking risks.
- Change to normal habits.
- Uncertainty.
- Being rushed.
- Acting without facts and a plan.
- Displays of emotion.
- Sudden changes.
- Making decisions.
- Having to socialise.
- Loud people.

Common bad feelings

Inadequacy — never having enough information.

Living with the Extreme Owl

Living with an Extreme Owl, like any other personality, can have its upsides and it's downsides.

The upsides are that the Extreme Owl is a steady, stable and reliable partner who is comfortable with habits and routines. They are family-centred, and responsible protectors and providers of those they care about.

They are the solid citizens of life — conservative and law-abiding. In a crisis, the Extreme Owl can be a pillar of strength.

One of the downsides is that they can be a bit of a boring stick in the mud, especially if they're in a relationship with someone who likes to socialise.

They also expect others to operate using the same rules and logic as they do, which can be an almost impossible task for the rest of us mere mortals.

Another downside is that while they may show patience with others, they can become sternly impatient with their loved ones, especially about their perceived character flaws and misdeeds. As a result they can become straight laced, critical and demanding, adopting a 'Holier Than Thou' attitude of "Why can't you be more like me?" This is their sharpest, and most used, Pygmalion chisel. This is especially true if they're in a relationship with a Peacock, who is the extreme opposite of an Owl.

They prefer to read a good book (alone) or carry out some job, or hobby, (alone) rather than mix, or socialise, with other people — especially strangers. So, don't expect to go to too many parties, or out to dinner too often.

But if you're looking for a good steady, reliable and responsible partner who will not give you too many surprises, you couldn't go past the steadfast and solid Extreme Owl.

THE OWL-PEACOCK PARTNER

"We are here to do our duty and to look after each other."

So speaks the Owl-Peacock stating the guiding philosophy of all Owl-Peacocks.

The Owl-Peacock is an interesting personality style. They have a happy mix of qualities. On one hand, they have the traits of the structured and analytical Owl, while on the other, they are outgoing and talkative like a Peacock.

Socially confident, they will strike up a conversation with almost anybody, especially strangers, and chat away as if they've known them for ages. And they can talk the leg off a chair!

Those who know Owl-Peacocks, often describe them as 'gracious, thoughtful, cheerful and considerate' — which they are — in spades. They are the most warm-hearted of all the types and always seem to be doing something nice for someone.

They were the kids who normally did well at school, often being described in their report cards as 'pleasant, helpful and hardworking'.

Gifted (or cursed?) with a strong social conscience, Owl-Peacocks pride themselves on being responsible and dependable to their families, their colleagues, and the community at large. 'Duty and Service' is the driving philosophy that guides their thinking and actions.

Their natural skills often find them in sales, teaching, lecturing, social work, the clergy, and the like. In fact anywhere there is a duty and service aspect, and contact with people.

Social creatures, they are people-people who are concerned with how others feel. Patient and forgiving of human foibles, they usually involve themselves with things that affect people's lives. Because of this, they are often involved in the community; on committees, in civic clubs, as volunteers, as elected members of the local council and the like.

They also make great salespeople, because they are generally comfortable talking to almost anybody (they can chat for hours on just about any subject). They put people at ease, they are considerate and genuinely helpful and they sincerely care about their customer's welfare; plus, they remember the names and personal details of most of these people.

They keep their ear to the ground.

They know what's going on — about everything and everybody. If you want to know the latest gossip, ask an Owl-Peacock.

Although outwardly modest, they have high personal ambitions and a quiet confidence about them that stems from a deep-seated belief in their ability to match, or excel, others in personal effort. They don't crow about this, they are just quietly confident about it.

They are usually extremely well read and skilled in some highly specialised (and sometimes quite obscure) area of expertise or knowledge.

Jovial on the outside, they are never the less great believers in Murphy's Law. Pessimistic by nature, Owl-Peacocks are inclined to take a negative and gloomy view of life. They generally expect the worst to happen, and are not backward in spreading the gloom and doom around.

They are very demanding of themselves and highly self-disciplined. As a result, they can be quite self-critical if they feel they haven't measured up to their own high standards. They are especially sensitive, and can be very easily hurt by anything that might sound like criticism.

In a nutshell

Owl-Peacocks are nice people. They are charming, jovial, likeable, devoted and honest. They care deeply about the welfare of others and are committed to not only helping those close to them, but the community as a whole.

Word portrait

Charming, friendly, gracious, talkative, energetic, enthusiastic, outgoing, sociable, warm hearted, unselfish, sympathetic, respectable, responsible, pessimistic, analytical, creative, patient, reliable, cooperative, popular, conscientious, discreet, pragmatic, precise, detailed, appreciative, loyal, considerate, perceptive, tactful, efficient, thorough.

Wants

Encouragement and praise

Admires

Those who do their duty.

Influences

They influence others with their confident, pleasant nature, and their reliability and loyalty.

Strengths

Friendly, honest, warm hearted, unselfish, gracious, and sociable.

Shortcomings

- Pessimistic.

- Can be over-efficient.

How they communicate

Great talkers, they can chat for hours (literally!) about almost anything.

They are askers, rather than tellers. Rather than being assertive, they will suggest using questions: "Have you thought about trying this … ?" What do you think if I was to …?" "Would you be upset if we were to … ?"

When you ask them a question, they will invariably give you 'the long answer' whether you want it or not. It has been said that when you ask them the time they'll tell you how a clock works!

Owl-Peacocks can give the impression that they know something about everything and sometimes this may convey a rather superior 'know-it-all' attitude without them realising it.

Under pressure

Owl-Peacocks want life to run smoothly and harmoniously. They shy away from conflict wherever possible.

When things don't go right around them they often take the blame, irrespective of whether it was their fault or not, and can become quite depressed.

When put under pressure, they become quiet and restrained, but if it keeps up, they are more than capable of expressing their discontent and letting the other person know how they feel.

They are often heard complaining.

They complain about being overworked and unappreciated.

They complain about aches and pains, constipation, and fears for their health in general.

Fears
Not being needed.

Basic Instinct
They are driven by the need to be needed and to do their duty.

Turn Ons

- Doing one's duty.
- Having a sociable chat.
- Helping others — being needed.
- Knowledge.
- Correctness.
- To be recognised and appreciated for what they do.
- Home improvements.
- Old fashioned values.
- Following routines and habit patterns.
- Socialising.
- Traditional celebrations.
- Well-mannered people, especially children.

Turn Offs

- Criticism.
- Not being appreciated for what they do for others.
- Conflict situations.
- Being overworked.
- Selfishness.
- People who are irresponsible.
- People who take a 'sloppy' approach to things.
- Constant aches and pains.

Common bad feelings
Gloom and doom.

Living with the Owl-Peacock

Owl-Peacocks take their job as family provider and protector very seriously.

Considerate, loving and deeply loyal, they stand by their partners through thick and thin, even if the relationship becomes rocky.

Orderly around the home, they expect the same from others, and look on selfishness and thoughtlessness as two unforgivable sins.

Compulsive nest-builders, they seem to be forever doing something to their home, or they're in the process of planning some future improvement.

Image and appearances are important to the Owl-Peacock. Having a 'standing in the community' — a good 'public image' is imperative. They believe in 'good old fashioned' values, and in 'doing the right thing'. They are dignified and well mannered, and want their children to be the same.

Protective and strongly devoted to their children, they do everything in their power to provide for their physical and mental well-being, and rarely spank them. However, if they're not careful, they can put too high an expectation on their children and get too wrapped up in their children's successes and failures, particularly 'failure', as they see it as a reflection on the whole family, and can become quite critical.

They build their lives on comforting routines and disciplines. Devoted to traditional values, they are guided by traditional 'shoulds' and 'shouldn'ts'. Although they are naturally kind, nurturing and caring, they can quite unconsciously use these 'shoulds' and 'shouldn'ts' as subtle Pygmalion chisels.

They enjoy socialising and entertaining and make great hosts and hostesses. They go to great lengths to make sure everybody is catered for, involved, and not feeling left out. Sentimental, they love traditional celebrations, anniversaries and birthdays and will go out of their way to make them memorable occasions.

If you are looking for a partner who is kind, considerate and loyal, and are prepared to spend some time alone while your partner is 'out there' doing good deeds for the community, then you can't go past the Owl-Peacock.

THE OWL-DOVE PARTNER

"I might sound old fashioned, but I think being respectable and doing one's duty is important."

So says the Owl-Dove speaking on behalf of all Owl-Doves.

The Owl-Dove is shy, quiet, soft-spoken and reserved. Their shyness is often mistaken for 'being a bit distant', but deep down they are warm, kind-hearted, and sympathetic people who are happy to give of themselves.

Uncomfortable in the public eye, and at social functions, especially with strangers, they are more than happy to blend in with the wallpaper while waiting for the time they can 'respectably' escape and go home.

The Owl-Dove's mission in life is 'To Be Of Service' — caring for the health and welfare of others — either those close to them or to the world at large. They want to make the world a safer and more caring place. Caring and compassionate, Owl-Doves will often put the needs of others before their own. Because of this, they are frequently overworked and taken for granted.

Modest and unassuming, they go about their day-to-day tasks without the need for public recognition or fanfare — in fact the last thing they want is to be put in the spotlight. But they do love a word of personal recognition and appreciation.

They were well-behaved kids and helped around the house when asked. They were also the kids who studied hard at school, knew the answers to all the teacher's questions, and never put a foot wrong. The word 'diligent' often appeared in their report cards. (And if work had report cards it still would).

They have a strong work ethic, and a deep sense of purpose. They take responsibility very seriously. Natural conformists, they seek a stable, unchanging sense of order and have a strong belief in social structures and authority. They also have a great respect for traditional values, rules and laws. Because of this, they feel most at home in jobs where long-established structures and procedures are in place, where everybody is expected to obey the rules and do things by the book.

They like to do one thing at a time and to totally concentrate on it, and will become flustered when asked to do several things at once. They write 'To Do' lists, otherwise they forget, so preoccupied are they on the thing they're concentrating on at the moment. The 'Absent Minded Professor' is often an endearing nickname put on them by those close to them.

They are lovers of history, tradition and keepers of 'old things' — furniture, photographs, family artefacts and the like. Tracing their family tree is often a favourite project.

Pessimistic, Owl-Doves are great believers in Murphy's Law. With an often-gloomy view of life, they generally expect the worst to happen and mentally prepare for it.

Mystical by nature, they are invariably strict devotees of a conventional religion, or certainly some belief system that fits in with their sense of harmony and order, and which helps to guide their thinking and actions.

They are often involved outside the home in some form of voluntary community work. They do this, as in all things, without the need for public fanfare. But what they do need is just a word of personal appreciation, which they don't often get, but that doesn't stop them from being there the next time they're needed.

Hire and watch the movie 'Iris'. It is a true story based on the life of Iris Murdoch, an Oxford philosopher and successful novelist, (and a Peacock-Dove) who was married to John Bayley, an Oxford professor, (and an Owl-Dove) for 40-odd interesting years. Not only is it a great story (and a real tear-jerker), but also both actors play their parts to perfection and give a real insight into the characters of a Peacock-Dove and an Owl-Dove. Interestingly enough, as was this one, relationships between these two styles are usually highly successful.

In a nutshell

Owl-Doves are steady, dependable, stable, quiet and modest. They are supportive, agreeable and tactful people who avoid any hint of conflict. They like harmony, order and structure in their lives, and for things to stay the same, both at home and at work. They are excellent team members and homemakers. Moderate and adaptable, they like to do one thing at a time and don't like to be rushed. They are loyal and conscientious workers, helpful and compassionate friends, and steady, reliable and caring partners.

Word portrait

Quiet, shy, friendly, calm, modest, passive, caring, honest, sincere, responsible, serious, conservative, dignified, sensible, stable, helpful, easygoing, pleasant, even-tempered, solitary, deep, compassionate, loyal, gentle, helpful, discreet, tranquil, considerate, tactful, diplomatic, harmonious, conscientious, thorough, painstaking, practical, reliable, accurate, ethical, altruistic, sympathetic, supportive, trusting, dependable, kind, peaceful, warm hearted, unassuming, sensitive, co-operative, precise, detailed, efficient, mystical, pessimistic, inhibited, withdrawn, fussy, staid, old fashioned, obsessive, evasive, hypersensitive, indecisive.

Wants

Wants the security of working and living in unchanging and familiar situations.

Admires

They admire people who have high standards and values.

Influences

They influence others through their consistency of mood, their steadiness, reliability, and loyalty.

Strengths

Steadfast, predictable and loyal.

Shortcomings

- Resists change.

- Over-cautious when it comes to unfamiliar situations.

- Depends too much on old habits.

How they communicate

Owl-Doves are non-assertive askers, not tellers.
    Rather than being assertive, they will advise and suggest.

They suggest using questions: "Do you think it would be a good idea if we were to ... ?" "How do you feel about ... ? "Would you be upset if we were to ...?"

They are also great listeners, especially for whatever ails you.

While they are quiet with strangers, with their friends and family they can talk the leg off a chair, going into the finest detail to explain what they're trying to get across.

Under pressure

Under pressure, they become tense and worried, and will quickly bend to whatever others want of them. They live by the maxim 'Do-anything-for-a-quiet-life.'

Under stress, they will keep their feelings to themselves and suffer in silence. And this long-suffering silence often shows itself in the form of headaches and/or skin rashes.

Fears

Taking risks. Changes to their set and familiar patterns. Conflict and disharmony.

Basic Instinct

They are driven by the need to be dependable, cooperative and respectable.

Turn Ons

- Being of service — doing one's duty.
- Helping others — being needed.
- Being appreciated and recognised for what one does for others.
- Knowledge.
- Following set routines and habit patterns.
- Law and order.
- Traditional family values.
- Harmony and order.
- Well-behaved children.

Turn Offs

- Taking risks.
- Change to their normal habits.
- Criticism.
- Conflict and disharmony.
- Being rushed.
- Doing many things at once.
- Socialising with strangers.
- Being overworked.
- Being taken for granted.
- People who don't take a 'serious' approach to things.
- Skin rashes.

Common bad feelings

Inadequacy — not having enough information.

Living with the Owl-Dove

Owl-Doves see commitment as a binding agreement, and are more than prepared to live up to that agreement. And they expect their partner to honour it in the same way.

They are extremely loyal and dependable partners who are comforting and easy to live with. Their driving force is family harmony and unity, and they do everything in their power to safeguard it.

Devoted, trusting, and patient, they are willing to put up with their partner's 'different' behaviour even though they may not approve of it, nor understand it. Of all the personality styles, the Owl-Dove is the least likely to play the Pygmalion Game.

The Owl-Dove's home is his, or her, castle. Natural nest-builders and homemakers, they run their home with the same meticulous structure and precision they like to do everything else. Orderly and organised, there is a place for everything, and everything is in its place. Deriving comfort and safety from habits, meals are served at the same time, and household chores are done in a set pattern and at regular times.

Because they watch their pennies closely, and seem to have a natural gift for it, the male Owl-Dove can, and does, put his hand to almost any handyman job around the house, including major renovations. And like everything else he does, it's done perfectly, even though it takes him twice as long as anybody else because of his perfectionism.

They are sentimental about the past and wish to preserve it. They will cling steadfastly to family history traditions, and especially love owning 'old family things.' They rarely cast off anything that has a link to the past even keeping things they had as children. And these will still be in perfect condition. As kids, Owl-Doves respected and looked after their toys — and always put them away.

With a pessimistic turn of mind ("What if ... ?"), they are 'sensible' with money. They know the value of a dollar and make careful 'family accountants.'

Reserved, modest and dignified, their innate shyness often prevents them from expressing their innermost feelings, especially words of love and affection. So they express their affection in action. The term, "Doing for others" was invented for the Owl-Dove.

They are strict protectors of traditional values and have a deep respect for a sense of dignity and decorum — doing the right thing. Keeping up appearances to the outside world is extremely important to the Owl-Dove. They are well mannered and so are their children. They live by high standards and expect their children to do the same.

Because of their protective and caring nature, they can be over-protective of their children resulting in them waiting too long before they 'fly on their own wings'.

They enjoy their own company and tend to keep themselves to themselves. Wanting privacy, they can get upset over unannounced visitors. So, except for close family gatherings, don't expect many parties. But if you're looking for a steady, caring and devoted partner who is not going to spring too many surprises on you, you can't go past the Owl-Dove to share your life with.

THE OWL-EAGLE PARTNER

"You might think I'm fussy, but I think it's terribly important to get things right, and I think everybody else should too."

This is the Owl-Eagle expressing the guiding philosophy of all Owl-Eagles. "Do it my way — the right way."

The Owl-Eagle is cautious, conservative and tough-minded. They have a strong belief in discipline and duty and take life very seriously. They are our solid citizens, our 'pillars of society'.

They are invariably well dressed and neat. They carry themselves with a rigid posture, have a serious face, and speak firmly. They appear cool and detached to those who aren't close to them. They are hard to read, and even harder to get to know. They keep themselves to themselves. They are compulsively punctual, serious and rarely, if ever, tell jokes. And if they do, they mess up the punch line.

Owl-Eagles have a strong belief in authority and care about doing things the 'right' way, respecting traditions, rules and laws. Their approach is often, "The old way is the only way."

Not very outgoing or emotionally expressive, they have a strong need for privacy. Physical contact is only given to a chosen few. But having said that, once they commit themselves to a loved one, they are deeply emotional, romantic, and passionate, and can be quite sensitive to any hint of rejection.

Loyal and reliable, with a strong sense of duty, Owl-Eagles are part of the solid aggregate that makes up the foundations of our structured institutions and who help keep them running along a set and stable path.

Realistic, conscientious, pragmatic, and principled — they live up to strict personal ideals and values. They approach most things with directness and integrity, and when not under pressure, are well mannered, courteous, and respectful. Perfectionists at heart, they are honest and fair people who have a hard time accepting their own and other people's imperfections.

Often referred to as the 'Guardians of the Status Quo', they feel most at home where there are long-established structures and procedures; where everybody knows their place and are expected to carry out their duties in the 'right' way, that is, by obeying the rules and respecting accepted procedures. They have little tolerance for 'inventiveness'. Precise, accurate and systematic, they hate incompetency in any form.

Their natural talents for being analytical, applying logic and taking a systematic cautionary approach often finds them in jobs as conservative businesspeople, lawyers, administrators, the public servants, military, teachers, doctors, the police, in fact anywhere there is a traditional structure and set ways of doing things.

Parental by nature, deep down the Owl-Eagles see it as their duty to show people the error of their ways, and have a 'blind spot' for naturally assuming that those on the receiving end of their advice or criticism will be grateful. And when they're not, the Owl-Eagle is surprised that their 'good counsel' has not been appreciated, or acted upon.

Strongly opinionated, they expect cooperation and are poised for confrontation if it is not forthcoming. Closing their minds to other peoples' ideas, opinions and suggestions, they tend to go through life sending the message, both overtly and covertly, "I'm right and you're wrong — do it my way."

Of course, quite often they are right, but many Owl-Eagles have yet to learn the two basic principles of being 'Right'. That is, firstly, there are many ways of being 'Right', and secondly, you can be 'Right' at the wrong time and in the wrong place, thereby winning the battle and losing the war when it comes to harmonious relationships.

Pessimistic by nature, and with their faithful attention to detail, the Owl-Eagle is always looking for the 'catch'. Cautious and meticulous, they never rush into anything. Risk should be avoided at all cost. Owl-Eagles want ironclad guarantees.

A perfectionist at heart, one of their favourite sayings is, "If you want something done right, do it yourself."

Rarely do they smoke, hardly ever drink — and never to excess.

In a nutshell

Owl-Eagles are conservative and analytical people who seek stability, structure and order in their lives. They are precise, accurate perfectionists who hate incompetence in any form. Disciplinarians, both at home and at work, they can be seen by some as cool, blunt, stubborn and critical when things aren't going their way. Self-disciplined, they are upholders of accepted traditions, rules, and social values.

Word portrait

Cautious, sensible, serious, organised, structured, systematic, analytical, logical, diligent, detailed, responsible, traditional, conservative, businesslike, dutiful, disciplined, perfectionist, pragmatic, practical, consistent, reliable, persistent, precise, accurate, thorough, straight laced, up tight, officious, fastidious, staid, stern, parental, impatient, intolerant, argumentative, pessimistic, bossy, picky, sanctimonious, dull, rigid, fussy obsessive, moralistic, righteous.

Wants

Structure, order and predictability.

Admires

Those who follow 'the rules'.

Influences

They influence others through their stable, logical approach and their self-discipline.

Strengths

Responsible, sensible, diligent, disciplined, determined.

Shortcomings

- Overuses criticism: "I'm right and you're wrong — do it my way" attitude.

- Over-explains — talks too much.

How they communicate

Tellers, rather than askers, they are the most outspoken of all the Owl types. While they generally prefer to be tactful and diplomatic, they are not shy in giving criticism.

They can be cool, blunt, critical, and stubborn.

They are quite comfortable when it comes to giving orders.

They offer their opinions (which they have on almost any subject), and are not backward in reprimanding others for any perceived misconduct.

When you ask them a question, they invariably give you the 'the long answer' whether you want it or not. It has been said that when you ask an Owl-Eagle the time, they'll tell you how a clock works!

Not particularly sociable, they like their own privacy and space, which can be seen by some as being aloof and withdrawn.

Under pressure

Under pressure the Owl-Eagle tends to become cool and critical, expressing themselves in short and brittle sentences that leaves no doubt as to their position.

They can often be heard saying, "If you want something done properly, then do it yourself."

They can also have a long memory for grievances, storing them up for later to be let out in anger in what (the other person may well feel) is a totally unrelated situation.

Fears

Change to the accepted way of doing things.

Basic Instinct

They are driven by the need for order, rules and structure.

Turn Ons

- Correctness.
- Being right.
- Doing one's duty.
- Neatness.
- Privacy and solitude.
- Traditional family values.
- Law and order.
- Being respected.
- Relying on structure, systems and habits.
- Taking the tried and proven approach.

Turn Offs

- Taking risks.
- Being wrong.
- Criticism.
- Taking an illogical and unplanned approach.
- Incompetency.
- Being rushed.
- People getting too close.
- Displays of emotion.
- Socialising.
- Undisciplined people.
- People who don't stick to the rules.
- People who take a 'sloppy' approach to things.
- People not following the 'the rules'.

Common bad feelings

An impending sense of failure and suppressed anger.

Living with the Owl-Eagle

Owl-Eagles are responsible, faithful, caring, and protective providers. As with all things, they approach their relationships with a deep sense of commitment, duty and loyalty.

They seek an organised, orderly and structured life. Neat and tidy people, there is a place for everything, and everything should be in it's place.

They are strict defenders of traditional values and strong maintainers of social rituals. They have a deep respect for a sense of decorum and propriety (being respectable), therefore keeping up appearances to the outside world is extremely important to the Owl-Eagle. They believe it should be just as important to all those close to them and expect the approved 'Rules of Conduct' to be followed by all in the family.

They care deeply for their loved ones, and in the privacy and intimacy of their own homes are not shy about showing their affection.

With their highly disciplined sense of right and wrong, coupled with their personal credo of "I'm right and you're wrong — do it my way", they can be energetic and outspoken Pygmalion chiselers who chip away at their loved ones and wear them down with "shoulds and shouldn'ts."

They see this criticism as only being beneficial to their partner and are quite unconscious of the effect it can have on their relationship, and may be quite surprised and taken aback when they're told it's nagging — which of course it is.

While in most situations they normally keep a 'stiff upper lip', in unguarded moments they can be quite sentimental, to the point of becoming teary-eyed while watching a sad movie, or in any situation that may touch their heart, which in most cases is normally kept well hidden.

If you are looking for a stable, loyal and conservative partner with a deep sense of responsibility and a great respect for respectability, you couldn't go past an Owl-Eagle partner to share your life with.

What a boring world it would be if we were all the same.

17

VIVA LA DIFFERENCE!

How boring life would be if we all thought the same way, if we all held the same beliefs, opinions and feelings.
It is being different that adds the spice to life.

Rather than struggling with each other, let's celebrate the difference.

LET'S APPLAUD THE PEACOCKS

Let's applaud and recognise the Peacocks for needing to have recognition and applause, and for entertaining us and making us laugh, and for constantly reminding us that life is too short to be serious. What a boring old world it would be without them.

LET'S CARE FOR THE DOVES

Let's make sure that we care for the Doves who need approval and belonging and who are the most compassionate, caring and supportive of people, and who constantly remind us that life is really all about loving and caring for each other. What a cruel world it would be without them.

LET'S ADMIRE THE EAGLES

Let's admire the Eagles for needing to control and for their no-nonsense approach in making things happen and bringing about change. If it weren't for the Eagles we would still be using the horse and cart. What a dull old world it would be without them.

LET'S RESPECT THE OWLS

Let's respect the Owls for needing predictability and security and thereby making sure that there is structture and law and order in our lives. What a chaotic world it would be without them.

Thank God for the differences!

18

LIVING AND LOVING FOR LIFE

BDBADA. No, it's not the name of a city in the Middle East!

It is the stages we go through (or don't go through) as we work our way (or not) towards establishing a loving and life-long relationship.

All relationships that start out on 'the rocky road to love' tend to travel along a fairly predictable, and more often than not, very bumpy path.

For some of us, the journey just gets too hard and we give up somewhere along the way. For others, they hang on in there but never quite reach the ultimate destination. And for others, the 'lucky ones' (Luck is a funny thing, the harder you work at something, the luckier you seem to get!), they hang on in there and finally reach their destination — a relationship where real love exists — for life.

Like any journey, when we know what signposts to look for, we will know what stage we are at in our journey. B-D-B-A-D-A are the signposts.

I call the journey 'The BDBADA Road.' The signposts are:

Blissful Ignorance
Denial
Bargaining
Anger
Depression
Acceptance

And the journey goes something like this:

Blissful Ignorance: *"This is the man/woman of my dreams — isn't he/she just beautiful!"* This is the first step of the journey — heart-pounding romantic love.

Denial: *"Nah, that's just a silly little habit that he/she will grow out of, if not, I'll help him/her to change."* The blinkers of romantic love start to come off. We kid ourselves that not only can we change our loved one, but also that he or she wants to be changed!

Bargaining: *"You know that funny little habit you've got, can we talk about it for a minute?"* Out come the small Pygmalion chisels, sharpened and ready to sculpt our loved one into the image of how we think they should be. The conditions start to be placed on our love. This is the, 'Why can't you be more like me' phase.

Anger: *"For God's sake, he/she has done nothing about it and it's driving me crazy! Enough's enough. It's time to put my foot down!"* Out come the big Pygmalion chisels in the form of criticism, cajoling, nagging, the silent treatment; the whole box and dice.

Depression: *"I can't handle this any more — what the Hell am I going to do — I'm at the end of my tether!"* This is the, 'Why can't the world conform to how I want it to be' phase.

Acceptance: *"I'm not going to change him/her. It's part of the package. After all, nobody's perfect — including me. I love him/her for all the qualities I admire and I'm going to forgive and accept those little things that irritate me. After all,* *isn't real love unconditional?"* Bingo! Acceptance. And more importantly, Forgiveness! Forgiving your partner for being who he or she is, letting your partner be just who they are, and loving him or her for it, and most of all — enjoying the differences, rather than fighting against them.

These stages are normal in any relationship that is worth having and nurturing. All couples experience it.

The cancer in a relationship starts to form when one, or both partners, get stuck in any one of the stages leading up to Acceptance — or they just give up along the way.

It can be a very hard road, but the destination is well worth the journey. Then again, doesn't anything in life worth having take time, effort and sacrifice?

WHERE ARE THE GOAL POSTS?

We plan our weddings like a military battle. Nothing is left to chance. Everything is organised with military precision.

The buck's night, the hen's night, the bridal shower, the invitation list, sending out the invitations, the wedding dress, the bridesmaids dresses, the grooms clothes, the best man's clothes, the flowers, the church, the cars, the photographer, the reception, the food, the drinks, the music, the going away clothes, the hotel, the honeymoon. Then what?

In other words, for most of us, we spend an awful lot of time and effort on what will last a day and only perhaps a few vague minutes on what we hope will last a lifetime; our marriage.

Having common goals is important, because they show us where we are heading. Without goals to aim for, life can be like spinning your wheels with no traction. The big problem with not setting your own goals is that life has an uncanny knack of setting them for you. And they most probably won't be the ones you finished up wanting. Life is too long not to do it right.

The clearer our ideas of what we are both trying to accomplish, both as individuals and as partners, the greater will be our chances of accomplishing them. The more we both face in the same direction, the quicker we will achieve them.

The following areas are a good starting point to setting some mutual goals:

- **CAREERS:** Who wants what?
- **INCOME:** How much is enough?
- **FINANCES:** Who handles what?
- **DOMESTIC DUTIES:** Who does what?
- **HOME:** How big? Where?
- **CHILDREN:** How many? If any?
- **SCHOOL:** Private or public?
- **FAMILY:** How often will you see each other's family?
- **FRIENDS:** How often will you see your own and each other's friends?
- **RECREATION:** What and how often?
- **RELIGION:** Can it be a source of disagreement?
- **OTHER:** Anything else that will need you both facing in the same direction.

A COMPASS FOR THE JOURNEY

Goals tell us where we're going.

Values tell us why we're going there.

Of all the couples I know who have a solid and enduring relationship, while they are all different in one way or another, the one thing they all have in common, their one common denominator, is that they strongly share and believe in similar values.

Shared values are the guiding compass in a relationship. No matter how hilly, or rocky, the terrain of life might become, our shared values — our compass — will always point us and guide us in the right direction.

Our values are the things we live by. Our values may even be something we are willing to die for. In other words, as a couple, our values are what we stand for. Because a relationship is such a tricky thing, if we don't stand together for our values, we might fall for anything.

Our values give life meaning,
  They're the things that we hold high.
They give our lives a purpose,
  They're the reason why we try.

Our values are our inner judge,
  They show us what is right.
Our values sift the shades of grey,
  They show us black from white.

When we question what it's all about,
  When we wonder why we try,
Our values give us reasons,
  They give our life a 'Why'.

Our values are our compass points,
  They're our map and guiding star,
They're at the core of our relationship,
  They make us who we are.

Shared values are always simple. They are never very sophisticated. ('Sophistication' is the art of making the simple complicated!). Here are a few that some of the 'lifer couples' I have met have shared with me.

- No matter what happens, we will never let a religious issue get in the way of our relationship.

- We believe that both of us should help out around the house, that is, we do not draw a distinction between who should do what.

- We agreed that we would have (x amount of) children — then stop!

- We believe that the greatest gift that we can give our children is our time.

- We will never let the sun go down on an argument. (An oldie, but still a goldie).

- We will never let the kids come between us, no matter what.

- We will have a dirty weekend together away from the kids at least every four months, no matter what — even if we have to beg, steal, or borrow the money to do it!

- We will not place our expectations on our children when it comes time for them to decide what jobs they want.

- We will try and instil strong values in our children, then give them the freedom and responsibility to make their own decisions in life.

Values, of course, are very personal and private things. And they are easier to say than live by. But, then again, isn't that true of anything that is important in life?

A RELATIONSHIP CAN BE HARD WORK

A good relationship just doesn't happen. It's something that has to be worked at.

As John Denver used to sing, "Some days are diamonds, some days are stones..." Anyone who has been married for longer than ten minutes knows that relationships are not all love and light, in fact they can be downright hard work. As a friend of mine said to me not long ago, "I reckon that living together is an unnatural act performed by consenting adults!"

A good relationship takes hard work and patience.

A good relationship takes time.

When we love something, we give it our time and attention. Watch any teenager as he lovingly polishes, tunes and generally dotes on his car. Watch somebody doing a hobby they love. Watch a gardener lovingly tendering their garden. When we love and value something, we spend time caring for it.

Our time is one of the most valuable things we can bring to a relationship.

Remember, 'Love' is a doing word.

THERE IS NO SUCH THING AS A "LITTLE THING"

The older I get the more I am convinced that there is no such thing as a 'little thing' in life, especially when it comes to a relationship.

Wars and divorces are caused through 'little things'.

Little things, both good and bad, add up.

It is as if we all have a personal 'Emotional Bank Account' that we keep. This account has a column on one side marked 'Deposits' and a column on the other side marked 'Withdrawals'. And like our bank accounts, we keep an eye on the balance.

When we have a positive experience in our relationship it goes into the 'Deposit' side, and when we have a negative experience, we put it into the 'Withdrawal' side.

A relationship flourishes when both partner's accounts are in the black.

A relationship starts to crack up and break when one, or the other of the partners, goes into overdraft!

YOU HAVE TO ACCENTUATE THE POSITIVE

It always amazes me how most of life's basic truths can be expressed in a simple sentence. And it also amazes me how when you read, or hear them, you get a 'blinding flash of the obvious' — well, I do anyway.

One day I had a blinding flash of the obvious when I read: *To be loved, you have to be lovable.*

How obvious is that? But is it? Like all basic truths, it throws up as many questions as it answers. What makes somebody lovable? How do you become lovable?

Going through my files the other day, (I tend to collect this sort of stuff as you might have gathered by now), I came across an article that could well answer these questions.

Firstly, I should say that I haven't got a clue where the article came from, but it's dated 1993, so I reckon the information would still be more than valid, but I'll let you be the judge of that. Here is the gist of it:

Based on a long-term study conducted by a group of psychologists at the University of Washington, they found they could predict with 94 per cent accuracy the fates of 52 married couples. And they predicted every single one of the seven couples that ultimately divorced with 100 per cent accuracy.

They did this by the simple act of counting the number of positive comments against the number of negative comments each person exchanged with their partner over a period of time.

In order to succeed, the researchers found, a marriage needed a ratio of five positives for every negative. That is, five compliments for each complaint, five expressions of affection for each outburst of anger or blame. Five good things for every bad.

The bottom line of the research is that people need warm, positive reinforcement from their partner in order for the relationship to stay on course.

This is not to say that anger and having a good old 'go in' now and again inevitably leads to divorce. In fact the researchers found a group of successful couples whom they labelled 'volatile'. These were couples who fought a lot, but who also loved a lot. The battles may have been fierce, but they ultimately conformed to the five-to-one figure. They gave each other five positives for every negative. Their marriages were successful in spite of the kinds of conflicts that destroyed other marriages because the overall balance was on the positive side.

You know, everything that goes round, comes round. There is on old song that has the line, "You have to accentuate the positive and reduce the negative..."

Perhaps using the five-to-one rule is a way of being lovable.

It would also certainly put you well into credit in your partner's 'Emotional Bank Account'.

I CAN'T LIVE WITHOUT YOU

All the happy couples I know have learnt that a true acceptance of their own and each other's individuality and separateness is the only foundation upon which a mature marriage can be based and on which real love can grow.

Two people love each other only when they are quite capable of living without each other — but *choose* to live with each other.

We all have a certain amount of dependency needs and feelings; we wouldn't be human without them. We all like to be taken care of now and again. We all occasionally like to be mothered and fathered. It's when these feelings dictate our lives that we have problems.

When dependency on another person totally dictates and rules our quality of life, psychologists call it 'passive dependent personality disorder', and it is perhaps the most common of all psychiatric disorders.

"I am nothing without you." When we rely on someone else for our identity, our self-esteem, our sense of self, then we are on a slippery slide, simply because we are incapable of loving another unless we first love ourselves.

Love for self and others goes hand in hand.

If we don't love ourselves first, then we become takers not givers.

I can think of no better words that describe the importance of independence in a marriage than those of the prophet by Kahlil Gibran:

> *But let there be spaces in your togetherness,*
>   *And let the winds of the heavens dance between you.*
>
> *Love one another, but make not a bond of love:*
>   *Let it rather be a moving sea between the shores of your souls.*
> *Fill each other's cup but drink not from one cup.*
>   *Give one another of your bread but eat not from the same loaf.*
> *Sing and dance together and be joyous, but let each one of you be alone,*
>   *Even as the strings of a lute are alone though they quiver with the same music.*
>
> *Give your hearts, but not into each other's keeping.*
>   *For only the hand of life can contain your hearts.*
> *And stand together yet not too near together:*
>   *For the pillars of the temple stand apart,*
> *And the oak tree and the cypress grow not in each other's shadow.*

From *The Prophet*, by Kahlil Gibran, copyright 1923 Kahlil Gibran.

TO BE 'HAPPILY MARRIED'

According to most research, if you ask young people on the street what their main goal in life is, most will answer, "to be happily married."

Yet the figures show that there is a better than 50 percent chance that when they do get married it will be a disappointing and painful experience. And if they try again, the figures show that their second marriage won't fair much better.

The truth is that making a relationship work places enormous stress on most people. It requires an incredible amount of work. To expect anything different is fantasy.

Marriage means having thousands of breakfasts together, worrying about paying the bills, going through all kinds of problems and crises together, enduring sickness, or depression, facing heavy disappointments together, watching each other get old, perhaps even one of you, as you get older, losing your mental capacity. That's when your partner needs to be your friend, rather than your lover — which is really what a successful marriage is all about.

CHOICES ARE OUR CHISELS

We are where we are today as a result of all the choices we have made so far.

One of the main messages of this book has been to show that there is no perfect mate, yet many of us waste much our lives trying to make our loved ones into who we think they should be. Rather than accepting, respecting and appreciating what makes our loved ones different from ourselves, we see the differences as shortcomings — weaknesses — and we then battle, both outwardly and inwardly, to try and narrow the gap between what our loved one is and what we think they ought to be.

We chisel away with our Pygmalion chisels. We try to carve them into an image of ourselves so that we can achieve some sort of ideal sameness. But it never works, and it never has.

When I become so engrossed in myself, so involved in what I want and need, it makes me blind. I become self–ish. That is why D H Lawrence's comment in his book *Sons and Lovers* rings so true when he says:

"The opposite of love is not hate, the opposite of love is self."

Let's put away our Pygmalion chisels and appreciate our loved ones for who they are.

The big message of this book is that the real task is to work on ourselves. We are the sculptors of our own thinking, not on someone else's. It doesn't matter what happens to us in life, it only matters how we take it. Choosing how we think is one of the few true freedoms of life.

We can choose our thoughts. Choices are our chisels. We can choose to be happy, or we can choose to be unhappy. The choice is always ours. The choices we make as to how we think are the chisels we should be using on ourselves — not on our loved ones.

Contentment is in our own minds. Anyone who thinks they can achieve happiness by changing anybody else's thinking but their own has little knowledge of human nature.

To think otherwise is to set ourselves up for a fall.

And finally, the main message of this book is that deep inside all of us is a very vulnerable and imperfect human being saying:

"If you don't understand me – then just love me."

Love is a choice

We choose to love, or we choose not to love.

Love is an act of the mind as much as it is a feeling of the heart.

When we put away our Pygmalion chisels,

When we accept that our loved one is human,

When we forgive our loved one for not being perfect,

When we love them for just being who they are,

When being alone together and enjoying each other's company is something you look forward to,

Then that is love.

19

RULES OF THE GAME OF LIFE

The following 'Rules of the Game of Life' is something I have had in my files for years.

I don't know where I got it, nor do I know who wrote it.

But I love it.

And as a final word, I wanted to share it with you.

Good luck.

Des Hunt

THE RULES OF THE GAME OF LIFE

1. You will receive a body. You may hate it, but it will be all yours.

2. You will learn lessons. You are enrolled in a full-time school called life. Each day in this school you will have opportunities to learn lessons. You may like the lessons or think them irrelevant or stupid.

3. There are no mistakes, only lessons. Growth is a process of trial and error experimentation. The 'failed' experiments are as much part of the process as the experiments that ultimately work.

4. A lesson is repeated until learned. A lesson will be presented to you in various forms until you have learned it. Then you can go on to the next lessons.

5. Learning lessons does not end. There is no part of life that does not contain its lessons. If you are alive there are lessons to be learned.

6. 'There' is no better than 'here'. When your 'there' has become 'here' you will simply obtain another 'there' that will again look better than 'here'.

7. Others are simply mirrors of you. You cannot love or hate something about another person unless it reflects something you love or hate about yourself. You envy that which you have not claimed for yourself.

8. What you make of your life is up to you. You have all the tools and resources you need. What you do with them is up to you. The choice is yours. You may start at any time to make your life what you want it to be.

9. Your answers lie inside you. All you need to do is look, listen and trust.

Author Unknown

ACKNOWLEDGEMENTS

The book you have just read is a better book than the one I originally wrote.

It's better thanks to the comments, suggestions and in-puts from my family and friends. A big thank you:

To my daughter Tracy, who like her mum, is a lovely Dove-Owl. She read every word of the manuscript, found some things that needed changing, liked what she read and encouraged me to forge on.

To my daughter Julie, an Eagle-Peacock like her dad, who read the manuscript, gave me her straight-to-the-point comments and also encouraged me to get going and get it published.

To Tracy's husband and my son-in-law Glen, a Dove-Owl, bordering on a Dove-Peacock, who also read it, liked it, and gave me his encouragement to continue.

To Julie's husband and my son-in-law Mark, an Owl-Dove, who used his great Owl analytical strengths and eye for detail to go through the manuscript to make corrections where he thought they needed to be made.

To my friend and colleague Peter McRostie, an Owl-Eagle, who made detailed notes and comments and concluded with "It's a good book" which is high praise indeed from an Owl-Eagle!

To my friend, and Peter's wife, Josie, a Dove-Peacock who read it three times, showed it to her family and friends, and told me to hurry up and get it published because it could help people.

To my friend Libby Sawtell, a supportive Dove-Owl who gave her time to go through the manuscript with a fine tooth comb and helped to edit out the kinks, even though she was shifting house at the time. Aren't Doves beautiful!

And the biggest thank you goes to Val, my lovely Dove-Owl wife who patiently looked at the same pages over and over again that I had written and rewritten for the umpteenth time and never once complained, and as usual, was always supporting and encouraging. Thank you my love.

It just proves again how much we all need each other.

Other Titles by Des Hunt

What Makes People Tick?
By Des Hunt
ISBN: 9780992555344
Genre: Non-fiction/self-help/personality
Publisher: AWC Business Solutions
www.tick.com.au

Available in print and ebook

This is Australia's quiet best-selling book and practical guide to self-discovery and personal growth. In it you will discover:

* Your own personality style and the style of those you live and work with
* How to see yourself as others see you
* The strengths, shortcomings and hidden talents of the different styles
* What style is best suited to what job
* How to pick another's style within 30 seconds of meeting them.
* How to relate better with others
* How to avoid personality clashes
* How to enrich your relationships

What Makes People Tick contains a unique, quick and easy-to-complete questionnaire to discover personality types as well as a Job Compatibility Indicator to pinpoint the most suitable personality type for each occupation. *What Makes People Tick* is 'must know' information for people who have to deal with, live with, sell to, and generally get on with other people.

www.ingramcontent.com/pod-product-compliance
Lightning Source LLC
Chambersburg PA
CBHW062126160426
43191CB00013B/2210